THE
ENERGY
FACTOR

ART McNEIL

THE ENERGY FACTOR

How to motivate your workforce

PIATKUS

This edition first published in
Great Britain in 1990 by
Judy Piatkus (Publishers) Ltd of
5 Windmill Street, London W1

First paperback edition 1993

First published in Canada in 1987
under the title The "I" of the Hurricane

British Library Cataloguing in Publication Data

McNeil, Art
    The energy factor: how to motivate your workforce.
    1. Personnel.   Motivation
    I. Title
    658.314

    ISBN 0–7499–1014–3
         0–7499–1237–5 (pbk)

Printed and bound in Great Britain by
Mackays of Chatham PLC, Chatham, Kent

To my family: Judy, Debbie and Karen who coped magnifi-
cently with my three-year obsession.

Preface

Energy...that's what this book is all about. Consequently, I am more interested in getting you to "do" things than "learn about" theory. Action, not knowledge, is the mission. I'll present a hurricane metaphor rather than theory, offer scrimmages for skill-practice rather than case studies for analysis, describe the behavior of great leaders rather than use statistics, and write in a straightforward style.

I developed my ideas in the midst of entrepreneurial activity, building my own consulting business, before returning to school to learn the academic perspective. I have worked throughout all levels of organizations, participated in many walks of life, lived in several locales, and associated with a wide variety of unique human beings. From this evolved my personal perspectives on energy and how you can create it.

Yours truly,

Art McNeil

Contents

Part One

Corporate Energy: A Survival Issue

Part One

Concrete Entropy:
A Survival Issue

1

Working Harder
or Smarter
Is Not Enough

What This Book Is Not

Senior executives have no interest in another variation of MBO (Management By Objectives), no time for yet another Big Plan. Executives have learned the hard way that organizational panaceas come at great cost and, historically, produce little return on investment.

Creating corporate energy is not like implementing a new technology or management system. Introducing new technologies and control systems takes time, time you probably can't spare just to learn new theory or a different way of accounting for things, and then there are months of waiting to see if there is a payoff. No one expecting to run an effective organization in a tough competitive marketplace will accept make-work projects.

And it's not just the time. Think back

13

to when one of your bosses attended a training course. You remember the problem: he came back all fired up, brimming with enthusiasm. Everyone was asked to learn a vocabulary of fresh buzzwords and adopt different ways of operating. But veterans survived — they dove under the nearest table and waited for a couple of weeks until the boss's enthusiasm wore off.

To act on the suggestions made in this book, you won't have to change your life or commit the organization to irreversible strategic decisions. You won't be asked to do anything that makes your staff seek cover under a table top. Nor will I ask you to scrap what has made you successful so far. You can significantly increase your contribution to corporate energy starting tomorrow, using current objectives, and without modification of your existing calendar commitments.

I hope to show you how to encourage your people to become more involved in *their* organization, to take the initiative and become innovative around the margins of their assignments. Working through this book will not require reams of analysis. No number-crunching. It is designed as an action plan that busy executives can experiment with. Introducing new management systems takes time and analysis. Creating energy on the other hand, requires action and visibility. So step back from your conditioned patterns of thinking for a few hours, and roll up your shirt sleeves.

The Catalyst Is You

Physicists tell us that energy can not be created or destroyed, and that any mass already has large quantities of energy stored in it. They explain that small applications of energy, properly administered, can liberate much greater amounts of energy.

No, you are not reading a physics text. I am, however, talking about creating and destroying energy — in this case, corporate energy. My experience suggests that vast reservoirs of energy exist in any organization — far more than most executives expect. It's just lying there waiting to be harnessed to a worthwhile enterprise. Your organization's energy may be as dormant as the atoms in the cover of this book. But it *is* there, waiting to be released by the correct stimulus. Organizations have the potential to tap a special kind of energy, energy that comes only when humans take risks and meet challenges head on. People experience this energy as exhilaration, vitality and a sense of urgency. This turned-on feeling creates a will to win, a desire to belong.

The creation of corporate energy involves everyone. Employees at every level, at every location and in every division have a part to play. It springs from something deep inside people that makes them want to work enthusiastically, with their hearts and heads as well as their hands. Corporate energy drives employee commitment to superb service and

It also requires a high amount of personal energy on the part of the leader. So make sure that you are "fit" to lead — and prepared to commit that energy to your organization.
David Clark,
President & CEO,
Campbell Soup
Company Ltd.

This is the first essential leap at faith; unless you really believe that energizing your organization will have immediate and significant impact on results, you'll probably fail.
David Clark

15

The analogy between physical and corporate energy is a good one, particularly if we extend it to the well-known "inertia" that inhibits change in large organizations. This seems to me to describe two different kinds of management problems. One is the inertia of stagnating energy levels. The other is the inertia of long-established success, which can ultimately be as destructive to the enterprise.

In a successful company, your people are already motivated and the organization has a momentum of its own. But what was the right direction (vision, goals, structure, corporate culture and strategies) for the last decade or more, may well be less than the best for the nineties and beyond. Then, it will take the full force of your leadership abilities to keep the company going like gangbusters, at the same time as you try to convince successful people of the necessity of change.

    John E. Cleghorn,
President,
Royal Bank
of Canada

when necessary empowers them to change the course of events for the better. When the vitality of an organization's people is focused and combined, almost anything can be accomplished.

Corporate energy fuels organizations to grow during good times and helps them to survive the bad. It is unleashed when a few people at the top demonstrate consistent leadership and are visible to their people. Effective leaders are the catalysts, the stimulus properly applied. But the catalytic role in high-performance organizations isn't restricted to those at the top. The real magic happens when leaders make sure that catalytic agents are dispersed throughout the organization. However, if the initial impetus from the top is missing, you won't necessarily be prevented from generating energy regardless of where you are positioned in the organization. A chain reaction can start in a single division, branch or production team. Starting in the middle is a much tougher assignment, but it can be done.

What organizations need most to win in today's fast-paced marketplace is people who possess skills that empower others; leaders who know how to inspire workteams to aggressively seek opportunities that will help their organization surpass the competition; leaders who can help others see potential solutions, not just problems; people who motivate others to rise above the status quo, see greater possibilities and constantly move the organization toward a vision, a preferred future.

When I work with executives, the issue of leadership invariably comes up. My first chore is to take the magic out of it. Leadership generally is assumed to be a trait managers are supposed to have. It is rarely taught, and managers feel particularly threatened when told they are deficient in it. The stereotype of a natural leader is the handsome, dashing and charismatic person, a dynamic speaker like Martin Luther King, Jr., or John F. Kennedy. Here were leaders who could galvanize a crowd, people who uninhibitedly willed the impossible to happen. But the energy that leaders generate around themselves does not exist because of mystical circumstances. Leaders are effective because they possess a set of skills — skills that can be learned. Of course, some will be more successful at generating and harnessing corporate energy than others. But everyone can and *should* work at improving his or her leadership skills.

People are hired for their technical competence, fired for their interpersonal incompetence, and promoted for their leadership skills.
Jack Zenger,
President,
Zenger Miller &
Associates Inc.

The High Cost of Efficiency

We had it our own way for a long time. Until the mid-70s, for a manager to succeed, all that was required was to keep his or her nose clean and do the job. If you followed your job profile and met the requirements of corporate auditors, you were guaranteed good earnings and job security. Companies just grew larger. Growth was assumed, and there seemed to be no end in sight.

Leaders who still believe that more of the same — like trying to become more efficient — will work are just building better dinosaurs. But as the Ice Age moves farther in, the efficient dinosaurs will be wiped out along with the others.
   Jim Clemmer,
   Executive
   Vice President,
   Achieve
   Enterprises Ltd.

Overconfidence developed because markets had been assured for decades and executives, spawned in this environment of affluence, seldom faced serious challenges. Senior teams devoted most of their time to drawing up long-range plans and postulating how wealth would be carved up amongst shareholders, management and labor. Wealth distribution, not wealth creation, was the order of the day.

When tough times arrived in the 80s, many senior officers found it hard to change. It was a shock to wake up and realize that what had made them successful was no longer good enough to assure organizational — or personal — survival. Markets and products began to change so quickly that managers could no longer rely on their systems, practices, policies and procedures. There just wasn't enough time or sufficient resources to tuck in all the loose ends.

Nature has an effective way of coping with redundancy, culling animal herds regularly, weeding out dysfunction to make sure that when a serious threat presents itself, the herd will be organized and conditioned to survive. Nature takes care to ensure that capable leaders and followers are in place. She sees to it that there is room and ample resources for members who demonstrate that they can do the job under fire. From time to time, individuals are asked to suffer in order to guarantee that fact, but group members know instinctively that the survival routine is in their own best interests.

On the corporate front, organizations, prior to 1980, had been without worthy predators for too long. With the challenges presented by shrinking resources, every organization had to examine what it was doing, to locate what was eating up limited resources and destroying energy. Leaders were forced to cull dysfunction. It took a while, but finally the message hit home for even the most passionate disbeliever. More of the same wouldn't work, and there wasn't time to wait for things to get better. Managing faster, better, or harder, wasn't good enough. Senior managers were literally forced to lead. Doing things right was not sufficient. Now, they had to also think about doing the right things.

In the past decade too many corporations have become entangled in policy and procedure, infra-structure and "analysis paralysis." They have ignored the most fundamental element — the human element — the relationship between the customer and the sales representative. Relationships, not transactions, build a successful business.
Will Barrett,
Executive
Vice President,
International
Operations,
AVCO Financial
Services Inc.

The Real Energy Crisis

As a leader, you are the one charged with unlocking corporate energy. And then you must pass it on. You're the quarterback who needs to be skilled at handing off the ball to those who will actually do the running. You've got to perform in such a way that your team's energy will be enhanced.

Yet when you look at the activities

management has historically concentrated on, you will realize that many of us have unconsciously behaved in ways that destroy energy. Senior managers often unwittingly diffuse instead of focus, confuse rather than inspire. It was the Greeks who first used words that specifically segregated work from other activities. In the past fifteen years the gap between those two aspects of life has widened alarmingly. Look at people who become visibly charged prior to a weekend, only to return to work with a case of the Monday morning blahs. Lack of energy and commitment is symptomatic of the reality that many employees perceive their jobs to be drudgery. Absentee statistics indicate that a surprisingly large number of disheartened employees don't bother to show up on Mondays at all. The sagging work ethic is a clear indication of the most serious energy crisis we face today: a shortage of corporate energy.

An interesting measure of corporate enthusiasm sits in the parking lot! In an organization where the "spark" exists, it's amazing to see the number of cars in the parking lot on Saturday mornings or much earlier than starting time during the week. The employees are here because they are "turned on."
Kenneth Field,
President,
Bramalea Ltd.

To succeed today, organizations must have energized employees who are in the "Saturday Mode" all the time. Before there can be a renaissance of the work ethic, leaders must find a way to get enjoyment back into the workplace. Employees need a chance to feel the exhilaration of personal success and accomplishment. The most rewarding aspect of my consulting experiences has been my discovery that being interested and committed is a natural state, a feeling within the reach of all human beings. But before it can happen, people need to connect with a catalyst, a leader who will activate their latent enthusiasm.

Successful organizational performance seems to go hand in hand with people being active, having fun at work as well as at home and in the community. We must have trained the brains out of our managers because business has become deathly serious. You'd think executives lined their people up every day and read the riot act: "If I catch anybody smiling or joking in front of customers, they're in for big trouble." Many managers genuinely believe that when employees are having fun at the job, they're automatically goofing off. So they intervene and demand more blood. They see their role as keeping everyone tightened up.

When things are going well, more of the same is all that's required. If an organization has already reached where it wants to be, efficiency-oriented positions like central staff teams, inspectors, and technically oriented middle managers are exactly what is needed. Affluence explains why management literature from World War II through to 1981 is preoccupied with strengthening the technical side of management. Yes! Management systems and practices made us more efficient. But they also relegated us to running our organizations by using only past trends such as financial reports and other output-oriented measures. And using reports to run an organization, particularly during

The more levels we have, the more possibility exists for us to become spectators.
T. F. Heenan, President & COO, British Columbia Telephone Company

rapidly changing times, is like trying to drive a car with your hands on the rear-view mirror.

Hindsight contributes little toward the production of corporate energy. When confronted with numbers in reports, managers are more inclined to spend time analyzing results and writing reports than they are in getting off their butts and making something happen. There is a difference between reading that the organization's service index is below average, and facing a human being nose to nose and hearing real-life complaints like "Your service is terrible." Folks on the firing line face visceral contact every day. But senior managers are protected. They live in an artificial bubble. Consumer noise seldom permeates the tranquility of a corporate boardroom. Most of our organizations' leaders have been trained as spectators — not as participants.

The Lesson of the Recession

The competitive race that organizations find themselves in today calls for high-performance drivers. If you tend to trend, if you are preoccupied with control systems or financial reports, you might survive — but only if you're lucky. Had Lee Iacocca listened to trends, he would have closed down Chrysler. The experts, management consultants, government agencies, and even union leaders, were reporting that Chrysler was dead in the water. But Iacocca, a lone voice of optimism, said, "Chrysler is not going to lose anymore, we're going to win." And he went one step further than talking. He behaved as if he really believed in Chrysler's eventual success. Every minute of his day, Iacocca behaved like a believer. His people could see determination and commitment in every action. Leader action and visibility are absolute necessities for the production of corporate energy. Action and visibility were eloquently displayed by Iacocca. Exposure helped people around him sense that miraculous things were happening. Iacocca's energy was felt; union leaders made concessions because they believed that, just maybe, there was a chance. Lending institutions put up money because perhaps there was opportunity. Government made tax concessions and loan guarantees because there was hope. One man's capacity to imagine success when the experts were saying "no way," saved a corporation. Sure, Chrysler received labor concessions. Yes, there were many rational factors that helped Iacocca pull it off, but the catalytic agent, the main ingredient in Chrysler's formula for turning things around was a leader who stepped out from behind the closed doors of his executive suite. He was not contained by Chrysler's existing systems, numbers, practices, or policies. He did not preoccupy himself with Chrysler's financial reports because he knew they were yesterday's news, and more bad wouldn't help.

To succeed, you've got to get your hands off the rear-view mirror and back onto the steering wheel. Organizations still need people who know how to use the rear-view mirror but the winners have senior managers whose hands are always on the wheel, leaders who know how to responsively guide their organizations. But leadership skills are in short supply. We spent years training leadership out of people. Our primary school taught conformity and business schools embellished the theme. I'm reminded of the story of a new graduate with a Master's degree in Business Administration who, after the ceremony, stepped onto the front steps of his Ivy League college and said, "I'm here world, and I've got my MBA." The world's response was, "Great kid, come on out and I'll teach you the rest of the alphabet."

The knee-jerk response of many managers to the problems brought on by recession was to install a new control system or seek a more efficient technological technique. They looked for solutions all over the world. There was an infatuation with Japan's statistical quality control. Managers looked everywhere except in their own backyard. Then, in 1981, Tom Peters and Bob Waterman, like the U.S. Cavalry, came to our rescue with an up-tempo message called *In Search of Excellence*. The authors provided a psychological lifeline for many managers who were dying on the vine, waiting for a survival strategy that would work. Everyone woke up to the fact that workable solutions need not come from distant places like Japan, but could also originate from their own bank of human talent. The spirit that made North America a rich, dynamic society is still alive, according to Peters and Waterman, albeit buried deep, beneath a burden of bureaucratic regulation, suppressed by rote-behaving senior officers and managers.

The most valuable man in the organization is not the most consistent, not the most courageous, not the most charismatic; it is the man that is most creative.
Will Barrett

The Proving Ground

My notion of corporate energy was developed and tested during implementation of an executive team discovery and action planning process called **TOWARD EXCELLENCE**™. A myriad of consulting experiences exposed me to many senior executives who were less than successful at creating energy in their organizations. The ones who were struggling were more comfortable delegating power to "things" than to people. They discovered that "things" don't respond well to challenge or change.

The post-war drive for efficiency (doing existing tasks better) introduced us to the use of management technology. The downside was that many people were forced to give up a degree of their humanness. Employees were often thought of as prisoners to, or extensions of, their respective machines. This attitude on the part of senior managers got so bad that by the 1970s it began to threaten economic survival.

Let me turn to nature's systems again to make a point about survival technique. Bees have survived for centuries through the good times and the bad. Their system obviously works. When a worker bee returns to the hive after a production trip, it walks a triangle. The apex of this triangle points directly to the source of pollen. The rest of the hive, trained to pick up on these signals, then fly a straight line to the source of pollen. That's where the term beeline came from. While the worker bee is doing his triangle dance, he also emits audible bleeps. The time interval between sounds indicates the exact distance to the source of pollen. Marvellous to contemplate. But the majesty of nature's design for the survival of bees is that only 82 percent are genetically capable of recognizing and following instructions. The other 18 percent are mutants, absolutely incapable of following directions. They're the explorers who fly off in error but, in the process, find new sources of pollen. Without these mutants, bees would soon deplete known resources and the hive would become extinct. If man were to create life, he would probably make one fatal mistake. He'd try to make life perfect which in itself would be an imperfection. Perfect systems eventually kill you.

Rote-behaving managers have good

intentions when they impose rigid rules, measures and procedures. But they leave no room for "screw-ups" and subsequently, the organization has no access to new ideas that may be accidentally stumbled upon. Systems-oriented managers kill enthusiasm and inhibit the judgment of those reporting to them. Judgment can only be developed by using it. Once operations become overly systematized and subject to excessive written rules, people no longer need to make decisions. In policy-driven environments, people become paranoid. They spend an inordinate amount of time covering their backsides, just in case something goes wrong.

A well-managed company is like a sailboat. It can have the best design, powerful sails, modern navigation equipment and a talented crew. But without wind (an energy source) all the skipper can do is stand on the bridge and flap the rudder back and forth. No direction or control is possible without energy. I've watched many well-managed sleeping giants spring to life when their leaders wake up to the necessity of corporate energy. Once turned-on leaders come into contact with their people, sails suddenly fill and the organization begins to move briskly and with purpose.

The ability to unleash the potential of your people is what distinguishes the true manager from the competent bureaucrat.
John Cleghorn

27

Finding the Right Balance

GOALS	VISIONING
DIRECTION (FOCUS)	ENERGY (POWER)
NEED TO ACCOMPLISH	NEED TO MOVE TOWARDS
MEASURED BY RESULTS	MEASURED BY FEELINGS
RATIONAL	INTUITIVE
CONSCIOUS	BELOW CONSCIOUS
ADULT MATURITY	CHILDLIKE CREATIVITY
LINEAR	HOLISTIC

Figure 1

Compare the two sides of Figure I which highlights the difference between management and leadership. The goal side provides direction which, in turn, fosters a need to accomplish the goal. Success is measured by results. The process is rational, and executed at the conscious level. The more experienced you are, the more logical your thinking. As our society developed its management side, we became more efficient. The price we paid, however, was a loss of the human magic that comes from the other side. We lost our ability to dream, to develop vivid mental pictures of different places to be or ways of being. The very term "to lead" implies having a different place to go to or way of being. How can you be a leader if you've got no place to go? And yet, organizations are filled with managers who have no vision. They are trapped within the real or imagined barriers and constraints of the status quo.

I don't want to downplay the value of technical managers and their analytical approach. Good management is vital to performance. Without it, opportunities would be recognized and talked about but never realized. But what is needed is balance. And to regain balance, most executives must strengthen the leadership skills of their management teams. North American managers already "know" more than they "do." Visible leadership can encourage action and provide a spark that will ignite corporate energy.

The question is where do we put people with strong managerial skills and where do we put managers who have strong leadership skills?
T. F. Heenan

The process of creating energy begins with senior managers but, for meaningful results, this energy must be transmitted to those who face the public. Nothing of consequence will happen until it does. Front-line performers are the only ones who can transform corporate energy into useful work. You gave up useful work for life the day you became a manager. Customers don't buy what managers make, so unless you are creating a productive energized environment for your people, you probably have become an unnecessary overhead. To involve workers you must strike a balance between management and leadership. Balance will allow employees to act like human beings again.

To keep your product or service on the

leading edge in a fast-changing world requires the input of every member of the organization. Before the advent of the assembly line, workers naturally had pride of craft in what they made. They had ungoverned opportunity to use their imaginations and the inventiveness to make improvements in their products. The challenge organizations face is to find ways to put both pride of craft and the natural inventiveness of workers back into the workplace. Very few of the advances we see around us resulted from middle management planning sessions or initiatives begun at the executive level. Most came from the front-line contributors who handled the product or faced the customer every day — people we now allow to use only their hands, not their minds or hearts.

Managers preoccupied with systems and controls often prevent ideas from germinating in the first place. The hands-on manager who jumps in to personally solve the problems of his department can be assured of only one thing: that the entire department will soon become dependent on him to solve its future problems.

When there are serious problems, managers with the quick-fix mindset will hire consultants to "turn the situation around." Unfortunately, the bigger the problem, the more senior management is inclined to believe that internal resources won't have the capacity to effect a solution. We suffer from the "Lone Ranger Syndrome." Leaders should be drawing on the talents, imagination, and experiences of their own staff members, rather than treating them like poor townsfolk, conditioned to sit back and wait for a masked man, complete with his executive assistant, to come riding over the hill.

I have sat on executive teams where management reports from the field were just numbers! numbers! numbers! When confronted with operating decisions, solutions always seemed simple. For example, the need to cut costs might be resolved by getting rid of a receptionist, the *person* at the front desk who meets *customers* coming through the door. A seemingly efficient management decision. But the spirit that keeps customers buying could well be cut to the quick by such action. Employees on the shop floor always knew that remote staff groups made more than their share of dumb decisions, a conviction that can destroy any remaining commitment to the organization. That's why it's imperative that the management of change involve people on the line who regularly face the public, eyeball to eyeball.

Executives, supervisors and managers need to get away from documents, they need to get outside of their systems so that those reporting to them can see a model of what's being asked for. It's easy to talk about change, but much harder to take personal action and be visibly supportive. It's harder still to be consistent when real problems occur and you have to act in a conditioned way. Once you recognize the power of observed executive behavior (leading by example) lots of recurring problems will get solved. Problems are often human rather than technical, and human problems are not usually solved by the use of statistics. Problems are more often overcome by getting out into the field.

Change is happening all around us. Organizations are much flatter. More authority is granted to workteams. Middle managers who perform in traditional ways are beginning to realize that they don't have a real job anymore. That reality hit home for me when, as director of sales and marketing for a telephone company which had been hit by a strike, I was asked to drive an installation truck. My five-year-old daughter remarked, "You must be doing okay, Dad. They gave you a truck." I tried to explain the relevance of my job as a director. I told her that I controlled, staffed, planned and directed. But all my daughter could relate to was that I wrote and talked on the telephone a lot. She was painfully close to the truth.

To stimulate the growth of new ideas you have to remember that when an employee comes to you with an idea — even if it sounds wild or pretentious — you must listen in a way that encourages him to come back. You have to free the minds of employees and win their hearts before the insatiable drive to improve performance will happen. You never know where ideas will come from or where they'll lead, but each one has the potential of being an energy source. At 3M, where

Anyone familiar with the tendency of field operations to blame head office for errors, omissions and "mysterious ways," will agree that this is getting right at the core of the matter. All management and head office staff positions are, or should be, a super-sophisticated support system for the people who are face-to-face with the customer in the field.
John Cleghorn

they have learned that mistakes can be profitable, if a project fails, no one is allowed to let it die. Other divisions must be apprised of why the project failed. Many times, another division will learn from the failure, and use it in an application quite different from what was originally intended. One person's failure, then, can become the germ of another person's success. It can happen in any organization that remains open to new ideas. To give you another example, during research and development on lead-acid batteries, a turned-on worker took home a container made from a new material. The container was left sitting on the kitchen sink where his wife saw it, added food and tossed it into the oven. And it worked ...that's how Pyrex got invented: like errors made by mutant bees, a productive accident. America's trip to the moon brought us many important benefits, most of them in the form of new technologies that were stumbled on through trial and error.

In 1984, we launched in-house task force sessions. Every quarter, six employees selected from any level and all operating areas are brought into our head office to tackle specific problems or opportunities. These small groups of people have been responsible for most of the innovation our company has seen in the past three years.
Until we introduced this concept we had no idea how much talent we had "out there."
Will Barrett

Leadership is needed not just to get us back to pre-recession strength, but to guide us through a world that will continue to change at an ever faster rate. Futurists tell us that we have entered an information age that will have an impact on us more profound than was the industrial revolution on our ancestors. At the turn of the century, technologies came along once a generation. Now major technological innovation can happen every three or four months. Time lines have shortened. There is less time available for rational and disciplined management procedures. So an alternative to management-by-control must be found.

A Strategic Map

Gaining commitment from executives to do something more than engage in philosophical debate about leadership and corporate energy challenged me to put the concept into terms that even the most rational of managers could work with. The result crystallized my ideas on the subject and may help you to put what follows into context.

(CE) creating corporate energy is a function of (V1), having a mental picture or vision of a place to go or way of being, plus (V2) an awareness of underlying core values that you and a critical mass of potential followers within a system believe in, times (SS) the use of skills to send consistent signals through day-to-day behavior in a manner that models personal commitment to the vision and core values.

Effective leaders accept as a given that (C) challenge is a legitimate responsibility of all organization members. When challenges are met with (ALR) appropriate leader responses ("appropriate" meaning consistent with the vision and core values), energy is available for transfer to task. The process of altering balance between (C) and (ALR) as a means of reinforcing

(V1) and (V2), therefore, is the essence of leadership.

$$\frac{CE f\ (V1 + V2)\ SS \times ALR}{C}$$

© McNeil 1984.

This is the most workable model of organization transformation and the achievement of excellence that I have seen.
Dr. Ronald Lippitt, Professor Emeritus, University of Michigan

The Basic Building Blocks

Core Values and Vision

Great leaders have always been able to discover core values and create an inspiring, congruent reason for being. They have built upon these a consensus for action, a working team. This combination provides the energy that will bind potential followers to a leader. The organization's core values and reason for being must be meaningful at the emotional level; they've got to tug at the heartstrings and make people want to belong.

Signaling Skills

Senior managers who are ineffective leaders fail because often they say one thing but signal contradictory messages through personal actions. Signals provide evidence to followers that the organization's vision and values are genuine. If a leader demonstrates by his own example, he will command respect. And when consistency

At Campbell Soup we remind ourselves that "You are what you do, not what you say you are."
David Clark

between the demands and the visible action of a leader exists, there is a greater likelihood that followers will paint themselves into the mental picture that has been created. They will transform the leader's vision into a shared dream.

Before the age of five, we learned most of what we need in order to survive as human beings. We learned what is really important by watching people in power. Before verbal skills were developed, we watched big people do things. As children we may have ignored what Mom and Dad said; we paid attention to what they did because we knew instinctively what was really important. In organizations, adults are at heart still child-like; they watch what their leaders do. And imitate that behavior. So, if executives isolate themselves in their offices, wondering if quarterly numbers will be met, odds are that middle management will too. You end up with an entire management team watching numbers rather than exercising leadership and making personal contributions toward improving performance.

The cold, hard reality is that organizations get from their management team the behavior role-modelled on a day-to-day basis by the executives. We have all been exposed at one time or another to the senior manager who gives an annual inspirational talk on topics such as the need to become market leaders, only to go about the remaining 364 days of the year checking expense reports, counting paperclips and acting in a manner that

Creating the vision is one thing. Ensuring that it is understood and remembered is another. Mentioning it to the group is certainly not enough. Developing it, then repeating it, and then living it is critical.
    Kenneth Field

signals everything but a genuine desire to be market driven. Employees quickly get the signal as to what is really important.

Challenge and Appropriate Leader Response

Management analysts may review your organization's statistics and relegate you to extinction. But if you can stay active and be out in front of your people, painting a clear mental picture of a future winning organization, if you give clear, uncomplicated signals, as did Lee Iacocca, people will eventually catch your drift and begin to make the improbable happen. Like signaling skills, a leader's readiness to encourage challenge and to respond appropriately when it happens, also has a multiplier effect. Each appropriate. leader response (meaning congruent with vision and values) made under fire, heightens corporate energy. Military leaders will tell you that soldiers respond better to leaders who have been tested under battle conditions.

Ineffective managers are already doing much of what is suggested in this book but from the wrong perspective. They send signals, but signals that are confusing and conflict with signals sent before. Core values may be present, but they remain untapped or, worse yet, have a negative influence on performance. Challenges arise but are avoided. The ineffective manager's inability to articulate a reason for being, plus the absence of vision doesn't send people anywhere, except home to find something more rewarding to do. As long as managers remain unskilled, they will lead their staff into low job-involvement and poor productivity, and they will secure the organization's inability to respond effectively to change.

It Was Trained out of Them — and it Can Be Trained Back into Them

For years I believed that a well-run organization was identified by its quiet and unruffled calm. Now I recognize that as an indicator of a dying organization.
       Jim Clemmer

If you've ever stood under high-voltage transmission lines, you know the sound of energy flowing. You can hear an identical hum in turned-on organizations. It's there the moment you step through their doors and meet one of their employees. It's broadcast to the world in their advertising and signaled by everything they do.

Each of the six dimensions of corporate energy can be practiced. Even to the untrained eye, meaningful results will be evident from the start. Most human beings have a natural capacity for some degree of leadership but it has been trained out of them. The leadership scrimmages presented in this book form a strategic map to take managers back, to help them re-discover the exhilaration and profitability that comes from the consistent use of leadership skills.

The greatest pay-off from creating corporate energy is that it will, in turn, create more energy. Passing on that energy to middle management and supervisors is crucial, because innovative concepts seldom originate in corporate boardrooms. Most ideas are spawned in the field, on shop floors, and in general offices. Without leadership, creative ideas never see the light of day.

The only way to put leadership into practice is to practice. This is no time for discussion, memos, or meetings. If you talk about leadership intentions, managers will be only too willing to take a vacation from their jobs and debate with you. Another "here we go again" response by managers will be to lie in the bushes and wait for your inevitable first mistake so that they can say, "I told you so." I'm not saying that creating corporate energy will be painless. As we learned during adolescence, change hurts.

Unlocking corporate energy requires a few people to exercise leadership in order to get it started. To be a leader, you must be ready to act, and not plan and analyse your team to death. It's like the story of the two brothers — twins — separated at birth. One was sent to Texas, the other ended up in Canada. Neither was aware of the other's existence until they were in their early twenties.

Finally, when they did re-discover each other, they decided to get acquainted by spending a weekend together hunting bear. When the time came, they drove to an isolated cabin. It was late when they arrived, so they left everything in the car and went to bed. Early the next morning the Texan landed with both feet on the floor.

"Where are they?" he demanded. "Let's get us a bear!"

The Canadian said, "Just a minute, the car is still full; we have to unpack, then we need to read our maps. We should check the compass, synchronize our watches, phone the forest rangers and let them know where we're going, then have some breakfast. We should be in the woods by 11:00."

The Texan got excited. "Let me at 'em right now. Just point the way."

The Canadian interrupted, "We don't even have the guns unpacked."

The Texan cut him off: "I don't care about the guns. I'll get 'em with my hands. Where are they?"

With great reluctance, the Canadian responded, "They're all around us..." But the Texan was gone before the sentence was finished.

About twenty minutes later, a horrendous scream was heard. Over the hill came the Texan with a brown bear at his backside, swiping and gouging. He reached the cabin, opened the door, sidestepped and let the bear tumble in. The Texan closed the door and shouted to his brother, "You skin that sucker, I'm off to get us a bunch more."

You may feel that I'm asking you to skin more than you can handle. But once you have a clear mental picture of what success would look like for your organization, once you start sending signals that are consistent with your vision, you're on your way. Perfection is most often developed on the fly. As the old saying goes: Life's a tough teacher because she hands out the tests before she gives the lessons.

Children have no hesitation to start something new. But adults are afraid of making mistakes. We are afraid because we are trained to imagine all the problems that could develop down the road. A friend's five-year-old son, fantasizing about being a cowboy, said that he would "ride" the couch until his parents could afford to buy him a horse. Follow his example. Start with little things at first. Use a couch until you get your horse. But you MUST ACT, or creating corporate energy will be just another theory, an additional overhead you don't need. New management systems take time and analysis. Creating corporate energy takes action and visibility. Your first step toward unlocking that energy is to take action — not make words.

Comments on People Who Create Energy

To help you understand how others have succeeded in doing what you are about to do, I have included profiles of people who have developed energy for their cause. It would be easy to paint a skewed picture in such brief summaries. But it is just as easy to distort in the opposite direction, imaginir g that heroes were bound to succeed, or that they possessed qualities and abilities beyond the reach of mere mortals.

An examination of the lives of the leaders I have profiled, and scores of others I did not include, shows the mystical assumption to be untrue. Many were average or below average students who took years to find their niche. They were not all gifted orators or public showmen. For example, Florence Nightingale was so shy of fame that she went into virtual hiding for two years after the Crimean War.

Many of these great leaders were also outstanding managers who often worked long, hard hours on administrative detail. Napoleon personally devised improved record-keeping and accounting methods, as did Florence Nightingale. The cost-accounting system she designed for the British Army Medical Services was still being used as a model for other government institutions eighty years later.

Another common trait of great leaders is their ability to attract bright minds from a variety of fields, fields they did not themselves understand. Churchill counted business leaders and scientists as well as political and diplomatic experts among his closest advisors. These strange bedfellows enabled him to stay several strides ahead of everyone else.

Historically, what great leaders have shared has been a carefully articulated set of core values that attracted followers and a clear sense of where they wanted to go. They signaled their vision and values with action and visibility.

Winston Churchill

Churchill had an illustrious career as a journalist, author, statesman and politician. He held a variety of cabinet posts in the British government from 1906 to 1929. When he was out of office for the ten years that followed, he had time to write and think deeply. This sabbatical, in his own opinion, prepared him for his role as an allied leader during the Second World War.

On September 3, 1939, Britain declared war on Germany and Churchill returned to the cabinet as first lord of the admiralty. Six months later he became prime minister. Britain and the other Commonwealth countries rallied around his indomitable spirit. He purposefully cultivated his "bulldog" image, recognizing that every public act was an opportunity to send a powerful signal. Behind the scenes, however, his time was spent coping with an enormous administrative burden. Perhaps his greatest challenge was the quiet diplomacy required to bring other countries, notably the United States, into the war. Without them, he knew he could not win.

France was overrun shortly after Churchill became prime minister. Germany counted on getting possession of the French navy. Churchill gave the French admiralty six hours to sail their ships into British ports or be sunk. It has been suggested that more negotiation might have won him the entire French navy without firing a shot. But Churchill wanted to show both sides that, unlike its predecessor, his government would stop at nothing to win.

"My policy is to wage war," he said in his first broadcast as prime minister. "War without stint. War to the uttermost." In the darkest days he painted an unshakable picture of a defiant unbroken nation that would go on fighting until ultimately victorious. Even before war was declared, he envisioned what would be needed to make victory possible. He understood the need for a build up of forces, for technological innovation, and for alliances with other countries.

Throughout the war he personified for a great many people the struggle to defend democracy and freedom from tyranny. He challenged people to make a unified effort. "Let us go forward together," was his favorite slogan. After the war, Churchill insisted it was Britain that had the lion's heart. "I had the luck to be called on to give the roar." But his contribution as a leader was undeniable. He was unusually effective and consistent in inspiring individuals to contribute well beyond their limits. Quite apart from his capacity to inspire, Churchill had the ability to organize masses of people. His clear directions left no room for the disorganization and confusion that reigned prior to his appointment during the first six months of the war.

Churchill's speeches contain many famous lines. The signal running through each speech was determination and defiance. He converted every public act into a micro-cosm of his nation's will to resist. He carried on with his personal duties in London during the blitz, making no concessions to danger, accepting the same conditions as the general public, demonstrating at every opportunity that he would not run from the enemy.

When Hitler invaded the Soviet Union, Churchill immediately began negotiating to win Stalin to the Allied side. Many of his Conservative colleagues spoke out strongly against any alliance with communists. Churchill, who had schemed for years looking for ways to overthrow the Soviet government, insisted that anyone prepared to fight Hitler was an ally.

_____ *LEADER PROFILE* _ _____

Values
- democracy and freedom from tyranny
- loyalty to country
- unity and cooperation

Vision
- victory of democracy over tyranny

Signaling
- "V" for victory sign
- the defiant and uncompromising tone of his speeches
- slogans like: "Let us go forward together."
- carrying on in London during the blitz

Appropriate Leader Response to Challenge
- firing on the French fleet
- negotiating with Stalin

2

The "I" of
the Hurricane

The Hurricane

In private conversation, executives frequently admit to me that they know they must find time to re-think their organization's primary strategies. They know they have to develop new insights before they can do a proper job of leading.

But there's so much going on. "How do I find the time?" they complain. Perhaps they are under pressure to explain why this quarter's performance is down, why budgets are over-run. Perhaps they are struggling to meet goals that no longer seem realistic, there doesn't seem to be enough time to handle even the day-to-day things.

Putting out fires is a full-time job. You face an uncertain market for your goods or services, stiff competition from cheaper imports, tougher legislation, new technologies that can make products obsolete overnight, and perhaps an unmotivated workforce. It's like being caught up in a hurricane. You keep waiting for things to get back to normal. In all that turbulence, how do you find answers? Caught up in it, you don't.

You can't escape the hurricane. The bad news is that there is no "normal" to go back to. What you are experiencing today is the way it's going to be from now on. Change is the only constant we are likely to see. And the content of the turbulence goes even farther than you may realize. It includes management systems, organization charts, policies, objectives, even the basic social training you received as a child — everything large or small that affects your actions.

I chose the hurricane theme because it accurately described what busy executives were telling me about what their jobs had become. But the more I researched this meteorological phenomenon, the more I saw the hurricane as a powerful metaphor that brought the concepts involved in creating corporate energy to life. It also allowed me to cut fifty pages of dry theory from the book.

General weather patterns are directed by the spinning of the Earth in what is called the corialis effect. This force, which makes water empty down a drain in a clockwise vortex in the northern hemisphere and counter-clockwise south of the equator, also controls weather everywhere on the globe. The effect of corialis is strongest at the poles and gradually reduces the closer you get to the equator. All weather is subject to this pattern, except hurricanes.

A hurricane is the only weather system separate from the global pattern. It stands alone, is internally motivated and can take a direction all its own regardless of what is happening around it. The energy hurricanes produce is staggering. Winds have been recorded as high as 190 miles per hour. The rate of heat-energy released inside a hurricane cloud-mass is in the order of one thousand times the amount of electrical energy generated in the entire United States in the same time period.

Hurricanes are created by the conjunction of two factors: water and warmth. In North America, hurricanes are born over the Caribbean where warm air masses draw up moisture, causing an atmospheric depression. This depression creates small waves that disrupt the general layers of temperature and pressure. It is these signals (disruptions of the status quo) that cause energy to center on them and thus create a new autonomous pattern. A hurricane spins, like a separate world with its own pole. It creates enormous energy and impacts everything around it.

The hurricane's energy is drawn from water vapor that is condensed back into water to fall again as rain, releasing what is known as latent heat. The heat rises, pulling in more moisture-laden air which spirals in to the center and rises to form a circular wall of towering cumulus clouds, releasing an almost constant deluge of rain. The associated release of heat encourages the air to rise still farther and faster.

By now the hurricane is like a nuclear breeder reactor. It can go on forever, unleashing enormous amounts of energy, as long as it keeps in touch with its source — the water and warmth.

The most powerful part of the hurricane is concentrated in a band of rain, cloud and violent wind about twelve miles wide and about nineteen miles out from the center. Farther out, tall clouds are more isolated, rain becomes showery and the winds less violent. In the eye, the temperature is warmer which keeps the pressure low and maintains the in-flow of air to the base of the storm. Within the eye, the sky is generally clear and winds drop to a gentle breeze. The roar of the storm beyond the cloud wall can still be heard, but on the inside it's tranquil.

The strength of a hurricane is that winds are focused on the eye. Everything is drawn toward the center. Only when the eye goes over land, losing touch with its source does the hurricane peter out and become part of the general world weather pattern again. If the eye of a hurricane remained just off the coast, if it remained in touch with its source of water and warmth, it could go on forever.

Briefly, successful organizations, like hurricanes, have a central core around which everything revolves and toward which everything is focused. At the center are ideas about what the organization believes in and where it is going. The hierarchy of an organization chart makes no sense in the "eye," where it's leadership and corporate energy that you're striving for. To tap the energy of managers and individual contributors, to organize them into a power source far greater than the sum of their parts, your organization must revolve around a set of core values that will draw your employees in and a vision that inspires the whole team with a sense of where the organization is going. Values and vision are to the organization what water and warmth are to hurricanes. They are the elements that leaders use to produce corporate energy. Once you lose touch with values and vision your organization's energy will dissipate and you'll gradually recede back into becoming part of the world's general weather pattern, reacting to the environment rather than having the capacity to select a direction all your own.

Organizations, like weather disturbances, are formed in a variety of ways. Many groups start out as winning combinations. They possess an internal energy that makes them world beaters. They start out with vision, a sense of purpose and clarity around what they believe in. New organizations possess great fury and excitement but, after a few years most lose touch with what gave them their energy. As they develop, they become preoccupied with systems, practices, policy and procedure — like hurricanes moving away

The most valuable resource with which executives work is not money, technology, buildings or equipment, but the energy stored up in people. Some executives unwittingly keep it bottled up inside themselves and others. The successful ones recognize that energy and set about pulling out the corks that keep it bottled up.
Jack Zenger

from their sources and drifting over land. They become part of the herd, struggling to maintain profit margins and market share. Once your employees, and customers, begin to lose sense of differentiation from the general flow, your business won't hold itself together. There just won't be enough energy. Innovation and creativity (disruptions of the status quo) happen only when vision and values are brought together. When these essentials are signaled to the organization, energy is produced. And as the skipper of the sailing ship without a wind to power it discovered, you need energy first before you can direct or control the craft. Good management, systems, policies and procedures, without energy, are worthless.

We have all seen organizations that failed to keep the "I" of their hurricane in touch with a source. They traveled a pattern similar to being out over a land mass, and eventually faded away.

Other organizations were blown around by prevailing conditions right from the beginning. They started with a good product or a new technology but without values or vision there was no energy to keep them alive. There is energy in a simple summer thunderstorm. But it doesn't last. And it has no capacity to control its own destiny.

The hurricane metaphor applies both to organizations and to individuals who have leadership skills and know how to get the energy-creation process going. Leaders signaling values and vision will

Once the core values and beliefs are understood, it's interesting to see what happens when an employee goes against the stream. The other employees want to ostracise the individual. They certainly let it be known that the person is not pulling his or her own weight or being a good member of the team.
Kenneth Field

start a chain reaction that will spread to the rest òf the organization. An essential leadership perspective is to acknowledge and accept the turbulence in one's life as being meaningful and necessary. Then you can start creating vision and discover your organization's core values. With these powerful tools, you can move through the storm of day-to-day affairs and reach your calm creative center — your own "I" of the hurricane.

Calm at the Center

At the center of every organization is a collection of ideas, beliefs and cultural traits. Whether they were put there deliberately and whether anyone is conscious of their presence, they exist and powerfully, but subtly, direct the performance of every employee. If no deliberate choice is made as to what belongs there, the organization's "I" will be filled with undesirable attitudes and behavior: wait for someone at head office to make the decision; hide the truth rather than be a bearer of bad news; get approval in writing before trying anything new; feel that quality doesn't matter, management just wants production.

Such energy-destroying attitudes become entrenched whenever an organization makes the all too common mistake of centering on its business plan. You have to understand that the policies, procedures and marketing strategies that are such an essential part of the turbulence, have no place in the creative "I." Quarterly sales targets have their effect in the right place, but if you build your organization around them you'll find that they don't have enough strength to keep all the rubbish out. The way to your center is to concentrate on a vision of a preferred future and the core values of potential followers. The "I" of the hurricane is a metaphor but the benefit of keeping your organization centered during the turbulence of day-to-day affairs is very real.

In winning organizations, values and vision do not change from day to day, because your month's sales figures are down or because there is a change in tax regulations, but nor do they remain entirely unaffected by what is going on in the turbulence. In the eye of your hurricane the breeze will be gentle, even though the roar of winds on the outside will still be heard. When centered you will be well aware of the turbulence beyond the cloud wall, but not controlled by it.

To gain insight into what will draw your people toward the center, and make them want to contribute their ideas and energies to the fullest, you have to become centered yourself. People who know how to use vision and values to find their way to the center of turbulence are resilient and have an amazing capacity to see new possibilities. The effect these centered people have on those caught up in the turbulence is powerful. Centered people are perceived as being sincere and human and this combination always commands attention in business as well as in personal life. I remember attending a business conference where a European delegate, unable to get a babysitter, brought her child to a pre-conference cocktail gathering. That tiny infant — with no power, without words of any kind — dominated the room. As the baby was passed from group to group, you could watch the behavior and vocabulary of powerful business people change.

The infant was centered. She used her longest and strongest suit — genuineness and helplessness. She was powerfully effective because her behavior was totally sincere and honest, completely in tune with her center. She wasn't intimidated by what was going on around her. Executives won't get much mileage out of acting helpless, but they can draw on their own unique qualities. If executives have a vision, if they take time to discover the core values of potential followers, they will be centered. Then, in their organization's turbulence, they can have the same quiet — yet powerful — impact that the child had on people around her. Centered people light up a room with presence.

To be centered was natural for us once, but it's not an easy state to recapture. The very young and the very old are freed from the hectic impact of turbulence. It's during the busy years between that people find themselves in the thick of merciless action. What differentiates a leader from others is an ability to accommodate that paradox: to fully live the busy years, while at the same time, using vision and the awareness of core values to tap the creative and inspiring benefits of a calm center.

Whether you are chairman of the board, manager, or worker, there needs to be a center of calm in your day-to-day turbulence, an area where the really important thinking can take place to make you a master of what you do. Once you discover this center, you'll be more effective at communicating with people around you. You'll find, through the example of your actions, that others will more easily discover their own centers, places where they will create better ways of doing things.

But don't make the mistake of cutting yourself off. The last thing effective leaders do is to turn off the hurricane. I've seen executives lock themselves away in an attempt to turn things around. It doesn't work. To be effective, you must be visible to your employees. You need to be present and involved, a contributing part of the turbulence or you will have little impact as a leader. Under fire, managers isolate themselves, whereas leaders will become more visibly part of the action. Daily, you need to make hundreds of microsecond trips, returning to your center, before reacting to challenges. There you can weigh the suitability of your habitual behavior pattern, then choose to react differently where deemed appropriate with an appropriate leader response.

Leaders, like artists, know the agony and vulnerability of being the lone advocate of an idea. Because of their trips to a center, they see possibilities before everyone else. The energy they find at their core gives them the intestinal fortitude to avoid being derailed by skeptics. As Peter Drucker, author and one of North America's most sought-after management consultants, remarked, "Anything of value in my experience has happened because of a monomaniac with a mission." Great leaders have the capacity to live in both the "I" and the turbulence. They are not sucked into permanent residence at either extreme — becoming philosphers at one end, or technicians at the other. They can move skillfully and instantaneously back and forth between the "I" and the turbulence. But for most of us, this movement isn't a natural act. It doesn't happen without practice and discipline.

Your All-essential "I"

No energy is created without someone to get the process started. Organizations need leaders who are prepared to take action. And their actions must be consistent with what they believe in. That way the signals being sent will have a ring of sincerity and integrity that people can believe in. To develop their trust, you must effectively communicate your insights to followers. That's the part that throws most people after they have been a senior manager for any length of time. Because of isolation, they're afraid they may have lost what it takes to get their point across.

Don't despair; to create energy you don't necessarily have to be a spellbinding speaker. Good verbal skills are a real asset, but speaking isn't the only means leaders use to communicate. You'll be judged just as much by your actions, and how consistent they are with where you say you want to go. And to be consistent day in and day out, you really have to know your "I," who you are at the center. In leadership terms, who you are is your vision, and core values. Your centre is contained in a secure package with only one link to the outside world: the signals you send through thousands of mundane daily actions. A leader signal is the only thing that followers see. It's what they are attracted to, and guided by.

It is a paradox of leadership that people want to follow the leader that they can trust to be behind them, ready to back them all the way.
John Cleghorn

I'm not recommending that you find a guru, or that you engage in a long bout of navel-gazing to discover the real you. You didn't get to where you are without having valuable qualities, personal dimensions that you use to send signals and connect with the people around you. Let's not complicate things unnecessarily. The "I," simply put, is the creative human being behind positions and systems, the person behind his or her things.

I've known many soft-spoken, reserved

leaders with incredible presence. Executives who use a limited amount of air time will be listened to more intently than those who are always on the podium. If you really have a place to go and something you believe in, you'll have no trouble getting your point across, both verbally and non-verbally. On the other hand, if you are uncertain about your destination, you'll communicate all right, but what will come across is, "Don't follow me, I'm not sure about where I'm going." To hone your leadership skills, I'll soon ask you to take what has always been your longest and strongest suit, rehearse in a low-risk environment, then run with it. The scrimmages section is designed for this purpose.

Core Values

This is where the metaphor should start to get real, where you start discovering your "I." The first step to unlocking corporate energy is to listen. On this issue, leaders must first follow. Leaders never create core values; they discover active or dormant beliefs that they and a critical mass of potential followers collectively care about. Then they shape or evolve them into a focus for energy. In too many cases managers see their staff more as machines with problems, than human beings with ideals and limitless potential. Humans have untapped energy that can be released by a catalyst properly applied.

There is a myth in most organizations that management is in control. It's far from the truth. People let managers think that they are in control. They may behave subserviently when the ineffective boss is around. But all he or she controls is their time — from nine to five. Employee hearts are reserved for things they believe in and can be proud of. These days, most people seem to take more pride in what they do outside of work.

In fact, real power resides at the bottom of an organization, not the top, if you accept as the definition of power the ability to actually do something.
David Clark

Yet people generally want to contribute more than they do. They would prefer to do work they could be proud of. Humans naturally want to believe in the organization they work for. Imagine for a moment that you are a middle manager in an organization with a poor record for customer service. Consciously or unconsciously, shoddy performance will be registered as a source of shame for you and your employees. Trying to motivate staff who are mired in a poor performance rut is impossible without leadership. You can't manage your way out of a performance rut. If a customer phones at five o'clock wanting a rush order, and you know that service is not something that anyone above or below you seems to care about, it's tough to believe that it's worth making the effort. You may be able to convince a work crew to fill the order, but your request may use up what little goodwill you've managed to build up with them.

But human energy is available even in the most lethargic organization. It's always there waiting to be tapped. No one intentionally sets out to do a poor job. If employees are convinced that their leaders really care about customer service — remember they need to see it before they will believe — pride of craft will soon replace shame. People will be found, eager to help you do the impossible. Everyone will begin to feel a sense of satisfaction each time a small performance improvement moves the organization closer to its declared values. Each time turned-on employees are called on to provide outstanding service, some energy is expended, but much more flows in to take its place. Energy is created rather than dissipated.

The core values that can produce that kind of response already exist in your organization, waiting for leaders to unlock and make use of them. These values may be well hidden, and appear non-existent. I've found that an easy way to spot a value is to look for sources of negative energy. I was working recently with the executive team of a packaged food company as they developed core values. Quality of product is usually a theme that companies want to get behind. But in this case they said, no. "None of our workers gives a damn about quality." The executives weren't happy with the level of quality being produced. It obviously bothered them. As soon as I sensed the depth of their frustration, I knew we'd located a

A human being without a set of values would likely lead a dismal and destructive life. A corporation without a set of values — employing thousands of people — would likely be a dismal and depressing place to work.

Will Barrett

powerful value. Today, quality has been declared a core value and it is lived hard. The difference is like night and day, at all levels of the company. Change took place because leaders started to demonstrate, through personal actions, their genuine concern for quality. Employees, once they discovered that executives meant what was being said, once they saw that their bosses shared the same values they did around the issue of quality, were delighted to pitch in and make quality happen. To outsiders it looked like a miracle. In reality, it was a predictable response to leadership. And everyone benefitted — consumers, employees and shareholders alike.

Think of the values you choose as a form of internal corporate advertising. By signaling values you are trying to win a position in the minds of employees, shareholders, and suppliers. If you pick the wrong values, you'll know it because very little will happen. But when you select a core value that is meaningful to you and your people, all kinds of positive action will start happening. Suddenly, people will become interested in your vision of where the organization is going. Seems overly simple doesn't it? Reserve your judgment until you try the scrimmages; my hunch is that you'll be pleasantly surprised.

Your first impression may be that I have made the leadership model too simple, that there are subtle but important nuances I've passed over. I've found that the concept has to be boiled down to its basic elements for two very important reasons. First, I don't want you to analyse and study leadership. That would play into the management trap and be dysfunctional. Action is needed to create energy; so an effective development plan should be simple, something you can start using tomorrow. Second, creating corporate energy is a collaborative effort. There are many others in your organization who will have to take part. You need something they can easily pick up on, and immediately put to use.

The CEO of a large telephone company called me at home one night. His executive team was uncomfortable with the documentation of a values statement they had developed. The executive team became concerned just before signing off final approval. In hindsight, the statement appeared too "motherhoodish" to them because it talked about service, integrity, quality and respect for the dignity of people. They wanted to "toughen it up" with some bottom line profit words. I asked the CEO what a corporate ad would look like that said, "We make good products, but we want to make a buck off you too." I mentioned that a values statement is designed to win the hearts of employees. It is not part of the business plan. Leave business plans out there in the turbulence, where they belong. Connecting a values statement with good advertising logic convinced his team and the CEO won his issue. The company endorsed a values statement that did not mention profit. An interesting footnote is that this company has managed to turn around a bleak profit picture. Although they did many things right, a large part of their success was a result of the values statement they selected. Their values statement turned people on.

Vision

"They can because they think they can."
Virgil

Once you've discovered values that will make your people proud to come to work each day, you've got half of your "I." But where are you going to lead people to? It is a serious yet often neglected question. You need to have a mental picture of a preferred future, another place to be or way of being, that people can buy into. You need something that inspires people and at the same time sets them free from having to ask for interpretations of policies at every turn. I am not referring to the familiar five-year plan, goals, objectives, or the much-needed analysis of strategic issues. Leave your business plans out there; they are essential but should be left as part of the turbulence. Business plans can scare people, or turn them off. They are not always suitable for mass exposure because of the cold hard logic they must contain. I am referring to word pictures that can bring business plans to life, declared "reasons for being" like Northern Telecom's "Towards the Intelligent Universe," Panasonic's "Slightly ahead of our time," or Bata's "Shoemaker to the World."

Helping executive teams develop vision taught me that the exercise becomes more effective when it is split into two components. First, a team must discover its "reason for being" — the other side of the coin from values. Reason for being is an abstract. It's not a business plan; there's no expectation to accomplish it. A good reason for being creates burning desire on the part of all employees to keep moving toward a superordinate target. This dimension of vision is used the same way navigators used the North Star. They never expected to go to the North Star. But they used it to get everywhere. Whenever your people get blown off course by the turbulence, a well-entrenched reason for being can provide a point of reference that will help them re-direct themselves as to where they're headed. Even if you have to radically change your business plan, drop product lines, or drastically alter organizational structure, your people will not feel abandoned if a reason for being exists. A sense of stability will still be there in spite of change. It keeps members focused on what is important.

Once you communicate that picture so that it becomes ingrained into the marrow of all levels of management and the

Vision can take dry statistics and make them over into an exciting, energizing dream that all stakeholders in the business (not just employees) can buy into.
David Clark

people who work for you, you'll find that you won't need as many rules and regulations. People will naturally understand what "fits" and what does not. You are providing a strategic map that frees them to be innovative. And because reason for being focuses the organization on preferred futures, it will also help people discover and eliminate a myriad of activities that are counterproductive.

Many organizations, unable to see a preferred future, are never able to go beyond where they are however well suited to rapid growth they may be in every other way. Northern Telecom was in that position in the 60s. Formerly Northern Electric, the company was a Canadian version of Western Electric, producing telecommunications equipment for Bell Canada, just as Western Electric did for AT&T. They had a comfortable relationship with Canada's telephone industry, with a gigantic share of the market. Management saw no reason to look beyond. But Walter Light who went on to become CEO, envisioned a world-class high-tech company and set out to make it happen. Resistance was strong from a traditional engineering community which included senior and middle management.

Initial ventures into world markets failed. Political figures complained about "our money" being thrown away on foreign ventures that could never succeed. But Walter Light persisted in his vision of a world class corporation. He accepted the flak and formulated a strong signal to

I've never read a more useful definition of the importance of knowing your corporation's raison d'être. Since we're all explorers of a turbulent present and a wide-open future, we can all benefit from Mr. McNeil's concept of having the "North Star" of the corporate vision to steer by.
John Cleghorn

Northern employees, shareholders and the market that there was no going back to being a big duck in a small Canadian pond. He changed the corporate signature to Northern Telecom, decentralized into autonomous divisions, and coaxed an ex-IT&T executive, John Lobb, to join his team. Lobb was assigned the mission of changing the attitude of Northern's management. Many of the corporation's sacred cows were challenged and managers who did not fit the new vision were released. Lobb's signals were the equivalent of Caesar's burning his boats on the shores of Britannia. There would be no going back.

Northern's reason for being evolved over the years into the theme "Towards the Intelligent Universe." It was a declaration that this company was destined to live on the leading edge of technology. This feeling of perpetual restlessness can be felt everywhere in what is now an extremely successful multi-national corporation.

But resistance at Northern Telecom is still present and the current leaders, like their colleagues in other successful corporations have a full-time job keeping the signal clear. No company can rest on its laurels. I recall consulting with a Northern Telecom company in Richardson, Texas. A big 250-pound recently recruited engineer asked me, "What the hell is an Intelligent Universe? If you can describe it, I can make it." He had not as yet grasped that the statement was a reason

Vision and reason for being have to start with actions. A slogan can enhance them but words alone ring hollow.
Jim Clemmer

for being, not a business plan or a product, but a strategic map designed to let everyone know where Northern Telecom was headed.

And it has worked. The corporation has successfully moved through several missions, each of which was appropriate for the particular market of the day. They've evolved from Telephone World to Digital World to what they call Open World (compatibility of different technologies) and I'm sure they will discover many future worlds.

The vision is lived hard at Northern Telecom. They have a system of quarterly operations reviews where each general plant manager is asked to present the status of his operation. Managers from other divisions have a standing invitation to attend these sessions to learn, challenge and contribute. The theme of all sessions focuses on "Towards the Intelligent Universe" or what have you done lately in the way of innovative technology or process?

The second stage of vision is the activity of visioning. It is the *act* of imagining the transformation of your reason for being into a working reality out there in the turbulence. Visioning produces the ongoing energy needed to keep you moving ahead. You ask yourself, "What could it look like?" Create mental pictures of possible futures and you might "see" what is needed to move closer to your reason for being. Before Jack Nicklaus drives from the tee, he runs an instant pre-play through his mind. He sees with his mind's eye exactly what he is going to do, every motion. He watches it all as if it were on a TV monitor, actually seeing the ball land just where he wants it to be on the fairway. I do the same thing, because every time I hit in front of a water obstacle, my mind sees the ball splashing into the middle of the pond. Most often mind maps become a self-fulfilling prophecy.

For a time I worked with an interesting human being by the name of Dr. Ed Lindaman. With a limited education, he earned an honorary doctorate, became president of a university, and was a director of program control for the manufacture of the Apollo spacecraft. Ed's mission on earth seemed to be to help a broad range of people to dream, to select preferred futures. A full ten years before Apollo reached the moon, simulated pictures of what the moon landing would look like were mounted on walls at Rockwell Standard, so that work teams would "get the picture." Every Monday morning via an in-house TV network, Ed would interview a different work team, often asking people to verbalize what the moon landing looked like to them. Apollo had hundreds of independent contractors working on the project. The flow chart in their project control room covered four walls, ceiling to floor. Ed's preoccupation with visioning helped him to mold potentially incompatible specialists into a productive team. He kept people focused on the vision. For example,

Somehow, executives have only lately realized the power of mental rehearsal in improving all their daily interactions. "Practice makes perfect," and all the practice can be done inside one's head.
Jack Zenger

when one engineer lamented about improving the performance of a part from one-failure-per-five-thousand to one-failure-per-five-million, Ed stopped the designer and said, "Before you get into telling me your troubles, what would it look like to you if this problem was resolved?" He kept everyone focused on a preferred future. It helped to unlock them when they were stuck. It provided the team with energy to keep trying even when the task seemed impossible. Ed's process of visioning drew the creative contribution of each contractor into a center. The process empowered them to do the impossible. It created a team out of individuals. The project remained centered because energy flowed between all the members. Ed personified what I mean by a catalyst.

Successful executives use visioning to begin the process of transforming what's in their "I" into a working reality. They imagine success long before the hard work begins, mentally rehearsing the act of reaching their destination. As children, great athletes and artists imagined eventual success. Mental pictures provided the energy to help them stick with the millions of hours of mundane practice that was needed to turn their dream into reality. But many who never made the grade also had visions of greatness. Visioning alone will not do it for you. If you don't have sound management skills and a business plan, it won't happen. What visioning can do is provide energy to carry you through the tough times when nothing else seems to be working.

When visioning, the mental picture you come up with will not always fit your organization's plans back in the hurricane. Don't be too concerned. All that matters is that your vision be worth working toward, something that you feel such intensity for that you will have the energy to hang on come hell or high water and eventually find ways of encouraging others to share your dream. Leaders are preoccupied with helping others buy into believing that a vision is worth moving toward. Leadership is an act of creation. Instead of simply allocating what is already there, leaders help people see what could be. Leaders help others to become what psychologist and bestselling author Dr. Wayne Dwyer calls "No Limits People."

Let's not make it sound easy. Once you have revealed your vision and pronounced your values, there is only one thing required to succeed — hard work!
Will Barrett

When an organization is centered on a vision, people will begin to trust one another. If you've ever had a new boss from outside the organization, you know what happens. For the first while no one tells him or her anything because no one is sure which way the wind will blow. Such distrust is a permanent feature for the working day of many people. It destroys energy and blocks creativity. But if the organization is centered on vision and values, everyone has a general sense of what will happen, and the resulting trust and mutual understanding break down barriers to the flow of energy.

Give your organization vision, a new

horizon. Remember, you already have a business plan to appeal to the head, and objectives for the hands of your employees; with vision you're after their hearts. You won't set people on fire with mental targets that can be reached in a year. If it's that close, you're presenting a goal. We are looking for something almost metaphysical. Vision needs to be spiritual in nature, something people can be constantly moving toward and striving for, but never feel compelled to reach.

Both phases of vision should be positive and uplifting, ideals that set high standards and connect with the emotions of people. When you leave your "I" and go back out into the hurricane, you will no doubt continue to worry about the next quarter's performance, but your vision will still be there, accessible to help you re-tune when the going gets tough or confused. You and all your people need to know that whenever they are blown off course by day-to-day affairs, they can step off the treadmill, sight into their organization's North Star, and reset the direction in which they want to move.

Go for some small early "wins" — small accomplishments that illustrate the benefits of practicing the core values. Then be sure to publicize and celebrate these early wins so that people can clearly understand what the core value means in practice.
David Clark

Vision is future tense, something you want to aim for. Values are what people believe inside, the right stuff that will make good things happen. Combined with the pragmatic grounding of your management systems and business plan you will be organized to succeed in our post-industrial society.

72

Sending Signals

Once you've successfully uncovered core values shared by a critical mass of your organization's employees, and developed a vision that shows people where you want the organization to go, how do you get the message out? You want people to see the connection between what they're doing and something bigger, something grander, but how do you make it happen? How do you start the energy flowing? You won't succeed by sending memos, holding policy sessions, or gala kick-off events. If you only talk about your vision and values, or make announcements about them, your people will sit in the bushes and look for ways to prove that it will never work.

People judge leaders not so much by what they say as by what they do. That's why creating energy takes action and visibility unlike the implementation of new technologies or management systems which takes time and analysis. Visibility means being among your people, not interfering with the content of their work, but aggressively living the organization's vision and values, saying things like, "I noticed you doing such and such. That's great because it fits with (your vision)." Leadership means visible activity. You have to find ways to say through your behavior what the organization is all about. Eventually, it will make sense to publicize your vision and values. But not at first. Live it for awhile. As noted advertising executive and author David Ogilivie said, "The three most important words in the English language are TEST, TEST, TEST."

When a leader is centered in the organization's turbulence, every behavior executed can, with a bit of thought, reinforce vision and values. In fact, every action you take already sends a signal about your beliefs, whatever they happen to be. Some are conscious, but most are not. This is the point where many executives in my workshops start worrying. And no wonder, when you consider the signals they've been sending. Many have a "loser's limp" syndrome. Have you ever noticed during a football game that if a player catches a pass, a herd of 300-pound brutes can grind him right into the dirt, and he'll still jump up and bound back to the huddle like an antelope? But if the same player drops the ball, even if nobody touches him he'll probably limp back to the huddle, check his equipment, adjust his contact lenses, and engage in all kinds of activity to prove that the reason for failure was out there, not anything within himself. Many executives signal that external reasons are responsible for their dropping the ball. Business is down and they're just not sure of the answers anymore.

Remember, even the five-year-olds know that it's not what you say that counts. Employees pay more attention to what you do. That's why I keep stressing that it's leader actions that create energy. The more visible you can make those actions, the more you will bring the values and vision to life, and the energy will start building.

If you think back to the powerful signal that John F. Kennedy sent about his commitment to defending Western Europe through his "Ich bin ein Berliner" speech, you realize it *wasn't* the words he used that created the impact. He could have issued a statement from the Oval Office and no one would have remembered. He sent the signal by going to Berlin — action and visibility — and his message was heard across the world.

The effect of signals is so powerful that it has a multiplier effect on values and vision, because they attract more and more people, and create more and more energy. Perhaps you've experienced the opposite: the multiplier effect of a dysfunctional signal, the act that turns off employees, like the lights going off all over an office tower at quitting time.

It's not easy to send signals that are always *consistent*, even if you strongly believe in them. That's why you must live values and vision. The essential ingredient to success is to be so visibly committed to the organization's vision and values that you send clear, consistent signals instinctively, regardless of the velocity of day-to-day turbulence. No one starts out being effective at signaling. You should practice signaling small items where no one will be too concerned if you should fail the first few times out.

As a leader, every behavior you exhibit either contributes to or detracts from your vision and values. That's why learning signaling skills is so crucial. Effective signaling has become an essential productivity key. Shorter life cycles mean there is less time and fewer resources available to create and manage complex control and measurement systems. Vision and core values communicated by the signals of your day-to-day behavior is a cost-effective alternative.

The more you practice and experience small successes, the more you'll find productive ways to make use of this invaluable skill. Pick something you would like to reinforce and jot down how many ways you could be visible in actively living it, within the confines of your existing objectives, calendar commitments, and personal management style.

A service business is going nowhere if it doesn't understand the world it serves. That is why, for example, a very significant part of the performance reviews of Royal Bank senior executives is based on their activities away from their desks — especially (but by no means exclusively) their client relationships.
John Cleghorn

I was working with the executive team of a large midwest company on the issue of leaderhip. They had begun the process of discovering what their core values were and had decided to send a signal about customer service. I pointed out why customer service was a tough issue. Service is a subject that executives are always concerned with but, because they do not handle customers directly, is difficult to signal. (Remember, it's only what people see that counts when it comes to signaling.) At first, the executives were stumped. What personal actions could they take that would demonstrate to their staff the importance of customer service?

The marketing executive was first to come up with an idea. He decided to ask each of his divisional sales managers to provide him with the names of their top two customers. He was going to visit them and discuss service. The signal was clear for all of his managers. The boss was going to see customers they hadn't talked to for years. Maybe it was time for them to get off their butts and do something about service.

It took longer for the director of finance to think of a suitable action plan, but eventually he deduced he would have lots in common with the financial officers of top customers and expressed a willingness to visit fellow comptrollers and talk about service. Once the customers were selected he began a round of personal visits and in each case the finance director experienced the same outcome. After a few minutes of polite professional chatter, the conversation always swung around to the problems that the company's billing method was causing. The director of finance went back to his office and said, "We've got to make some changes. Our billing ·system is causing serious problems for customers." Not surprisingly, reports were already in the system concerning poor customer attitudes about the billing system. But no real action happened until the director made a personal connection. Energy is created when leaders get back in touch with the real world of customers, suppliers and competitors. There is something different about reading a sterile report on service and having a real live client (who is also a

Employees may listen to your words and be impressed, but they're not going to follow you anywhere until they are impressed by your actions.

Will Barrett

professional colleague) tell you face-to-face that your service needs to improve. Visceral people-contact causes humans to "feel" and act; reports, by contrast, are more inclined to make people think and analyse.

In the early stages of a corporate culture change, it is necessary to be overly simplistic and overly direct in the signal that you send. Constant reference to the desired behaviors and/or outcomes is necessary to clearly, constantly and consistently illustrate what the core values should mean in practice. What you are striving for is the "Aha! That's what it means!" reaction from large numbers of employees.
David Clark

Every action you take sends a powerful signal. Few executives realize the power that their personal day-to-day behaviors (signals) have on others. To be effective, leaders need to use every means at their disposal to communicate. You'll find that mistakes are invariably the result of conflicting leader messages, perhaps sent years ago, that are still rattling around and causing trouble. Signals have a life of their own. Once they've been sent they keep on moving until someone with authority challenges them. Signals from senior officers move quickly. The signals you send today will probably spread through your organization before you get back to the office and empty your mail basket.

Challenge

North American culture teaches us to view challenge in threatening terms. Given half a chance most people would build a bureaucracy to protect themselves, rather than face challenge alone and vulnerable. But if you're interested in creating energy the last thing you should expect — or want — is to be isolated or connected with robot-like, yes-men employees who follow blindly and unquestioningly. If this is what your senior managers are doing, their commitment is in essence non-existent, and at the first sign of challenge, they'll delegate upwards or abandon ship.

I've had executives say that being prepared to accept challenge and respond appropriately was so obvious they wondered why I bothered to include it. The opposite is what should be obvious. We've all known of bosses who were "converted" to a new approach only to drop it at the first sign of crisis. That scenario is so common it has become ingrained as part of our business culture.

You can spend months getting people excited by values and vision, gradually convincing them that your interest is for real, and then kill the energy by one response to challenge that doesn't fit. When you start the process of creating corporate energy, employees may wish you success but there's only one way to convince them in the long run. Be ready to stick with your vision and values and send consistent signals, however great the challenge.

Challenges may come from extraneous factors like changes in the cost of raw materials, or the sudden appearance of foreign imports. But don't become dependent on challenge from outside. You have to invite and encourage challenge from within. And it's not just good business practice; it's an essential part of the survival process. You signal your desire for employees to start using their heads by letting them be creative and experiment with ideas around the margins of their assignments.

Dissatisfaction is another source of energy we must learn to harness, particularly creative dissatisfaction. Our people know the rule: "If you don't like it, show us a better way and let's fix it."
Will Barrett

Celebrate challenges that question what you are doing, recognize them not as threats, but as symptoms of potential strength in your organization. People resist because they don't want failure. Although some of their behavior may be misguided, dissidents usually have the organization's best interests at heart.

Leaders can't accomplish much on their own. To be a leader you must engage in collaborative efforts. If you're leading people, they will demand the opportunity to contribute to the organization's vision, embellishing it in any way they can. When people are really tuned in, they challenge. Welcome that challenge. Look for ways to make allies of resisters. If you don't pay attention to dissenters, the signal you're sending is "I don't want you to think." I'm the only one who has sufficient brain power around here to understand the situation." And you'll breed bureaucrats, you'll receive memos from them at every turn, asking for clarification on every initiative you want to take. Set an example that frees your people to be creative and initiate for themselves a degree of leadership. They can become valuable energy creators.

Appropriate Leader Response

Executives, like all human beings, are always making choices between wealth (long-term) and cash flow (short-term) strategies. This is also true in personal relationships, both in business and private life. On meeting someone for the first time, you subconsciously measure your actions with questions like "Will this encounter be a one-time meeting or a potentially long-lasting relationship?" The response of great leaders has always leaned away from the short term of cash flow toward wealth and longer-term strategies. When you sacrifice vision and values for short-term gain, you signal that they don't matter, and without consistency, followers lose energy. The leader's credibility is reduced with every inappropriate (not congruent with vision and values) response.

Making an appropriate response while in crises is the acid test of leadership. Playing the part is easy when things are going well. But once the shooting starts, you soon find out how good leaders really are. That's why practicing your signaling skills on a daily basis is so important. Appropriate responses must become second nature; they need to become so ingrained that in the face of challenge, your response will always be compatible with and supportive of your organization's vision and values. Once you establish a track record of consistency, subordinates will begin to trust and follow you, even when they aren't sure where you're headed. You will have signaled that you are a leader worth following.

Many executives are leading from a vacuum. Without vision and a sense of values their signals often confuse people. Business plans and economic thrusts (for example, profit) fail to excite anyone. Their personal responses, when challenged by subordinates, produce negative energy, labor strife and certain death to the possibility of their receiving new ideas from employees. In short, the absence of vision and values in organizations turns people off. There is no center to their turbulence. There is no leadership.

Only experience will teach the skills needed to create energy; so, if you want to be among the few leaders who will successfully shape their organization's future in a tough post-industrial age, start practicing your leadership skills. Find your reason for being, imagine the impossible, discover shared values and then really live like you believe in them. Start behaving as though the improbable is indeed possible and watch the magic happen around you.

Thomas J. Watson, Sr.

When Tom Watson joined the Computer-Tabulating-Recording Company, it had debts of $6.5 million and combined assets of just over $2 million. By the time of his death thirty-nine years later, IBM sales had increased more than a thousand times over to become one of the largest corporations in the world, with earnings larger than giants such as the Ford Motor Company and General Electric.

During his first several years as General Manager, Watson had problems with directors who wanted to form a stock pool to artificially inflate share values in order to collect short-term profits. Watson opposed the attempt because it was contrary to his vision of an international business with operations in every country, a company that could go on expanding forever by concentrating on excellence in execution, sales and product development.

By 1924, with the old directors gone, he renamed the company International Business Machines, and had completed the creation of an entirely new corporate spirit and identity which he himself epitomized. He was a master at dramatizing and simplifying the points he wanted to convey through the use of slogans and songs. An IBM school was started, to imbue new recruits with the philosophy of the organization so that it could be perpetuated decade after decade. "THINK" was what employees were asked to do; loyalty to IBM was expected.

Watson actively encouraged the retelling of anecdotes about his manner of handling situations so that managers in his ever-expanding empire could keep the process going. Whenever Watson spotted a new employee breaking IBM's unofficial dress code he would offer to advance money to enable the person to buy the "right" kind of clothes; managers looked for opportunities to emulate such methods.

IBM created a cult around employee equity, encouraging employees to assume company shares in lieu of increased salaries. As IBM's share value escalated, many employees grew rich in the process. It was part of Watson's vision of a company's being one big family which every employee would naturally want to be part of.

Businessmen of his time had little use for academics and, although Watson had little technical expertise, he knew intuitively how to make their research fit his vision. In the 1930s he became captivated by the idea of producing a tabulating machine that could operate at the speed of light. When researchers told him that the notion was impossible, he gave a $1 million grant to Harvard University and asked them to develop the first electro-mechanical computer. They succeeded, although the machine was fifty-one feet long and weighed two tons.

Throughout his business career, Watson kept a relentless personal pace, spending much of his time traveling from one IBM location to another, always disseminating his values and vision. He was able to evaluate every step the company was taking because he never lost touch with where the organization was going, or what it believed in.

_____ *LEADER PROFILE* _____

Values
- excellence in execution, the the best service in the world and respect for the dignity of the individual.

Vision
- IBM as a world organization that would go on forever
- business machines that operated at the speed of light

Signals
- the company anthem — "Ever Onward"
- IBM Day once a year, when thousands of employees came to one location for inspirational speeches, songs and meetings with senior management
- IBM country clubs
- hiring special trains named "Scientific Specials" to cross the country carrying IBM engineers and technicians who had completed training

Appropriate Leader Response to Challenge
- opposing stock manipulation in the early days
- paying to have the first computer developed when "experts" said it couldn't be done

3

Values and Vision:
A Blueprint

Values and vision are to an organization what water and warmth are to a hurricane. Together, they are the basic elements for the creation of energy in your organization. Once developed and entrenched in the "I," your corporate energy can be limitless. All that is required is to stay connected, to keep everyone in the picture. When an organization is centered on its values and vision, willing customers will surface like old bass, and employees will demonstrate time and again that they want to contribute. The urge to excel will become insatiable.

Developing values and vision to the stage where they can be enshrined on a wall plaque will take time — I've worked with companies where the process took a full year — but you don't start by making declarations. Wordsmithing is reserved for the end of the process. It is the icing on the cake. You can start tomorrow practicing your skills with small-scale tests, experimenting to find what works for you. Even though your initial attempts will be small and preliminary actions may fall wide of the mark, I think you're going to be surprised at how much energy you *can* create.

Looking Within to Find Values

There is no rule that says you have to first discover values before going on to develop vision, but most of the people I've worked with find it easier that way. Eventually, your organization will settle on two or three core values. All you need to begin your energy-creating experiments is to temporarily select one value that you can believe in.

The most common core values that organizations put to use are:

Selected Most Often

1. Service
2. Respect for people
3. Quality of product
4. Innovative capacity

Honorable Mentions

5. Honesty
6. Competence
7. Reliability
8. Value added
9. Trust
10. Winning

Variations on these themes are used by organizations all over the world. They are expressed in such slogans as "Quality goes in before the name goes on." To make core values work, you must discover what binds people to the organization and use it to create your own corialis effect.

Simple Steps to Discovering Values

1. Reach deep within yourself for something that you obsessively believe to be true.

What is it that impels you to come to work each morning? It may be people — customers, employees or the larger community. Or is it to make the best product or provide superb service? Whatever your attraction, take hold of it and look at the organization around you. How will the majority of people respond? If you can't unequivocally say, "I feel strongly. And I believe most of my employees will too," then go back to the drawing board.

2. Pay attention to sources of negative energy.

Think back to when you noticed evidence of frustration from co-workers when quality, service, or respect for people wasn't there. Look for what's already in your organization. Leaders don't create values: they discover and nurture them.

3. Ask old-timers what it used to be like.

What fired people up decades ago?

4. Talk to customers.

Rediscover what they like about your organization. There are lots of things you're doing right even if you are not always conscious of them.

5. Research and study the organization's early records.

The people who got your organization started — your pioneering entrepreneurs — probably had a neatly distilled sense of their new venture's values and vision. They may not have talked about it in these terms, but they were undoubtedly centered on a belief or vision that pulled them through the tough years. Even after a century, original values can be rattling around the corporation, waiting to ignite the same excitement that your founders had access to.

To clarify the complete list of core values, you may want to play with all of these approaches. But for now, all you need is a single trial value that you can quietly begin testing. It may not be the one you finally settle on, but don't worry. You're not going to make any announcements. You won't be making commitments that you'll have to go back on.

For employees, the motivation to accomplish high performance occurs when clear signals are sent, signals that are uncomplicated by extraneous or conflicting notions, and when senior managers begin to indicate through their personal behavior how deeply they feel the expressed value. To keep the energy flowing, and growing, an increasing number of signals will be needed, and they will have to become increasingly visible.

Testing Your Trial Value

The next chapter contains a series of scrimmages that will allow you to experiment with the value you choose. When you hit on a workable core value, you'll know. Energy destroyers will be pushed out of your "I." People will become less concerned with empire building, covering their butts, and performing for executive attention. There will be a new vitality connected to the job. For years experts said that employees wanted only more money, and that people were in business just to make a profit. Managers were too well-trained to believe naively in motherhood notions such as employees getting motivated by the opportunity to deliver outstanding service. Being called at midnight to help solve a customer's problem seemed too much to ask of the Me Generation. It *was* too much to ask because senior management, through their actions, signaled that they only valued profit, even at the expense of customer service. Managers had a cash-flow or short-term mentality; long term wealth was assumed.

But profits, as the past decades have shown, are not

enough to motivate people or organizations, not powerful enough to fill the "I." When you aim for profits, you become the same as every other organization. Nothing differentiates you from competitors or, for that matter, corporations in other fields. No wonder college graduates in the 60s and 70s had so little enthusiasm for business as a career, and so much trouble choosing between particular corporations. They had all become the same: part of the general pattern. I don't believe that human beings have changed that much since the days when pride of craft was important to tradesmen. Employees will still go that extra mile and feel better for having done it, if their trip supports a value or vision that they believe in.

The Strategic Payoff

The search for values is not a make-work project. To hardened executives it may seem like a "soft" activity, but the energy it releases can have a powerful impact on your bottom line. Three years ago, a new president was hired to turn around a division of a multi-national packaged food company. For a long time it had been run as a branch plant operation with a new leader parachuted in every two or three years. Rather than taking the most common approach in turnarounds — firing the senior people, and cutting costs to achieve short-term profit — the new president chose the higher risk route of interacting with the organization's people at all levels. He discovered that year after year the company had been deviating from its traditional emphasis on quality. They hadn't lessened public appeal for their product but the employees' sense of pride in what they made had slowly been whittled away. The employees' commitment to producing top quality products was still present, but it was creating despair and distancing them from their company.

I can recall working with the corporation's senior team as they went through the process of rediscovering values. One executive said very little. He was a rough, tough-line manager who ran a mushroom operation — one of the few departments that managed to maintain profitability during a period of overall corporate loss. With each new president, this executive had fiercely defended his people and their method of operating, insisting that they grew "the best damned mushrooms in the world." During the dialogue, a colleague from another division turned to the old-timer and said, "I'm beginning to see that this getting-back-to-basics stuff is what you've been harping about to us all along. That's what made you successful over the years while we were preoccupied with playing at the latest management fad."

While this discovery process was going on, the company didn't put their day-to-day business on hold. Profits went up despite an industry slump. They became leaders in new product innovation and, whereas three years before their shift, they had trouble recruiting talent, now people of the highest calibre are knocking on their door. A turnaround happened because this president worked obsessively with his people to make core values a visible part of their everyday turbulence. Executives from this company still tell the story about how their employees have made it happen. By involving people at all levels during the rediscovery process, an enormous amount of pent-up energy was released.

The creation of a system of cascading values through the various levels of the organization is the most essential and most difficult stage in this rediscovery process. It requires relentless continuous effort. What begins as the lonely pursuit of a leader must ultimately involve everyone. I worked with the executives of an organization that for years had been unable to agree on a values statement. Fortunately, what they believed in was already understood by employees. The commitment theme — "we do what we say we will do" — was so firmly entrenched that people had been hired and fired because of it for years. When this company announces that a new technology will be ready for the market at a certain date, it is. It's a consistent source of pride for everyone who works there. So don't lock yourself in a boardroom to create the right value. Get out and interact with real people. Experiment and you'll soon discover your energy source.

Start from Where You Are

Values, properly signaled, have their greatest impact when they first come from senior executives, but that shouldn't prevent anyone in the organization from starting the process at his or her own level. Let's take that beleaguered middle manager with the poor service problem again, or a supervisor of a secretarial pool. Assume that they both employ staff that lacks commitment, demonstrates boredom, and displays poor work habits. They could institute more controls, such as timing employee trips to the washroom, counting errors, or issuing tighter policies. But that approach only tackles symptoms. At any level of the organization, you can find values that will motivate your direct reports, bring meaning to their work, and give them something to be proud of.

Vision

Years ago, I worked for a manager who was advised late in his career that telling employees what to do prevented them from achieving their full potential. His response was to stop telling us anything. No one knew what he wanted. And for months, everyone in the department wasted half his or her energy trying to divine what the boss really wanted. People perform better when they know where the finish line is. Vision, like objectives, gives people a sense of direction, but unlike objectives it leaves employees more freedom to move in their own way.

The capacity to envision seperates human beings from other creatures that share this planet. The strategic relevance of visioning is that our mental scenarios of possible futures influence in a concrete way the limits we put on ourselves. As the late Dr. Edward Lindaman stated, "A fundamental determinate of how we choose to behave is our conscious or below-conscious expectation of what the future could hold in store."

Parents will readily concede that children are not advocates of Murphy's Law. Unfortunately, this naturally optimistic outlook is often subdued at an early age because of negative feedback received from well-intentioned adults. Experts suggest that during our early years the ratio of negative to positive input averages 12:1. Constructive criticism is in reality negative input. For example, "Why don't you do it this way?" implies that the child is wrong and in need of help. The consequence of our early exposure to negative feedback is that when left to our own devices, we often find ourselves in a creative vacuum, entertaining visions of what *could* go wrong, dark images of impending doom.

The familiar themes recur during internal dialogues. Messages such as "I've tried that before, I could never do it", or "It's too risky," are symptomatic of this defeatist attitude. Unless they consciously work at it most adults, when challenged, will imagine only the worst possible scenario because their subconscious minds have been programmed to do so.

Vision contains two distinct elements. These elements

may eventually merge so completely that you will be able to see them as one. But, for now, keep them separate.

Reason for Being

Getting executives to entertain the notion of reason for being is a struggle. The trouble is that they don't understand the concept. "I've no time for motherhood stuff", is a typical response. They don't see what reason for being has to do with running a railroad. When they first enter the "I" it's strange for them. Getting them in is tough; getting them to stay is tougher. Creating reason for being seems far removed from the results they're searching for. The potential for increased performance through the use of reason for being comes as a *gestalt* for most managers. It's like a joke; until they get it the whole thing seems pointless. Only when they see the connection, when they literally picture it in their minds, do they get the message. Marilyn Ferguson, in her best-selling book *The Aquarian Conspiracy*, called this mental process a paradigm shift.

When I ask executives to imagine what they are moving toward, their first response is often to come up with a new product or achieve a certain profit margin. Until they can let go of their business plan they'll never get beyond the problems of today. But if executives commit themselves to the process they will invariably come up with something powerful. Often they don't recognize how powerful their reason for being is at the time. It's when executives return from the "I" with vision established that "Ahahs" start to happen. Converts begin to see all kinds of solutions that weren't previously visible to them. They make connections between ideas they've never even considered.

Options for Creating Reason for Being

1. Complete these statements:
   In a Utopian setting,
   Our customers will see us as −
   Our shareholders will see us as −
   Our competition will see us as −
   The way we're treating ourselves is −

2. Have a slogan campaign.

   Pass out cards to employees, asking them for two sentences on how they see the organization. Involving others creates excitement, and a feeling of ownership.

3. List the things you're not.

4. Study previous corporate advertising.

   When I work with a group of eight to ten executives, I divide the group into two and ask the members to fill up wall charts with visions of preferred futures. I allow them only a short time period so that their management-conditioning and preoccupation with perfection won't kick in. After five minutes of brainstorming they note common themes and begin visceral discussions. The results will typically come in slogan form. To create energy you have to paint a picture using metaphors and words that contain meaning for people in your organization. Executive teams I work with are often surprised at how easily they reach consensus on reason for being. It is not like business plans where everyone struggles to protect his or her turf.

A Word about Wordsmithing

You start with the concept. The perfect phrases will come soon enough. Corporate energy is not produced by the wording but by the unceasing tenacity displayed in signaling.

Most managers believe that their organization knows where it is headed. I have not found that to be the case. Senior executives often aren't sure themselves. But to succeed, corporate targets must be understood by every employee. There is a child's party game that starts with writing out a message and whispering it from one child to the other until the last one announces the transmitted message to the group. By the time everyone has translated and passed on what they thought they heard the resulting garbled version bears little relation to the original. Most senior executives have been whispering their vision when they should be signaling it with a personal touch, frequently and visibly.

Reason for being must be kept in front of your people at all times. I was invited by Tom Bata, chairman of Bata International, a privately owned multi-billion dollar corporation, one of the world's largest shoe manufacturers, to participate in an executive development meeting. During volatile table discussions, I watched talented executives reaffirming the heart of their business. The company's reason for being was already clear to them. Their leader came from several generations of shoemakers and his father once said, "I was put on the face of the earth to shoe mankind." To this day the reason-for-being statement at Bata is "Shoemakers to the World." That theme has produced sufficient energy to propel Bata to establish itself in over eighty-five countries around the world. But Tom's executive team recognized that they had to be vigilant to prevent bureaucracy from interfering. I was impressed with how determined they were to stay with the basics.

The wonder of a powerful reason for being is that it's the stuff of great legends. There is a story in the Bata organization about an employee sent to conduct a marketing survey in Africa. He returned saying, "There's no market. Africans don't wear shoes." Every year in North America, countless new ventures are considered — and discarded — with this reasoning. But such a negative conclusion wasn't acceptable to a manager totally committed to the Bata vision. When he heard the report, he said, "You mean to tell me you found people who don't have shoes and you can't see a market opportunity?"

Such legends live long. They can shape and frame the culture of an entire organization. Legends are very effective at keeping reason for being alive. Think about it. People don't usually talk about IBM equipment. Their stories are more often about uncompromising service or respect for people — values that IBM people have lived to the fullest over the years.

Visioning

The process of visioning is designed as a beginning. But people don't use it because they have been trained to be results oriented. The payoff from visioning happens out in the turbulence. Inside the "I" is where you play with possibilities, knowing that once you can mentally see the preferred future, everything in the turbulence will start to center on it and you'll drive out counterproductive activity.

The reason-for-being aspect of vision is an abstract. Business plans alone won't keep you slightly ahead of your time. You need energy to make plans come alive, and that's why you should practice the fine art of visioning. It is an essential profitability key in today's marketplace.

Creativity is being able to function within a paradox. As any artist knows, it's hard to do. Nothing but raw guts and determination holds an artist together long enough to make his or her insight a reality for the outside world. Visioning can give your organization that same energy. Excitement will happen when suddenly people get the punch line. Having a *gestalt* will often remind an adult of what it was like when he was a child. Oh to get back to imagining, to see and play with possibilities as if they were actually there.

If you can imagine something vividly, you will probably eventually accomplish at least a variation of it. In the "I," you envision the kind of future you want to make happen back out in the turbulence. We've all waited during olympic games while, for what seems like ages, a high jumper goes through a mental rehearsal — a visible moving picture of a successful jump framed in his or her mind. Great athletes succeed mentally before making a real world attempt. They know that they must see success in their minds before the human body can be expected to perform at a level of perfection. The four-minute mile is another example. It was thought to be impossible — until Roger Bannister broke the record, removing a barrier to performance — and now even high school athletes run the mile in under four minutes.

An interesting experiment on visioning was conducted with the co-operation of a college basketball team. One third of the players were told not to practice free-throws, another third was asked to practice frequently, and the final group was told to imagine making perfect free-throws for the same interval as the second group practiced. Researchers were overwhelmed to learn that it was the visioning group who most improved their performance.

Practice doesn't make perfect, as Vince Lombardi, the great football coach once said. Only perfect practice makes perfect and your mind's eye is one place where with a little discipline you can attain consistent perfection.

Humans have been blessed or cursed, depending on your perspective, with a very important vacuum between their ears. This void fills with mental images of possible futures whether we like it or not. The only choice we have is to consciously fill our vacuums with pictures of preferred futures, or let nature take its course and be content with reacting to the random chatter of whatever our subconscious mind serves up.

Your vision will cause many irreversible changes in the organization. Imagine what could happen if every employee understood where you wanted to go and was eagerly striving to make it happen. How different is this conjecture from your present reality?

Give yourself permission to have some fun; leave your systems, plans and objectives out in the turbulence and start brainstorming. When visioning, the ideas will come pouring out, and with them, energy and excitement. A midwest electronics company executed 87 percent of the commitments made within sixty days of an executive team visioning session. The president was amazed. That level of energized activity with a complete management team was completely outside his experience. It was made possible because of the energy that a shared vision released.

Using the visioning process, one team of executives from a dencentralized multi-billion dollar conglomerate evolved an image of "acting like five." Recognizing that they were out of touch with the corporation because they had grown too large and diverse, they imagined what it might be like for each of them if they tried to run their large company as though they were executives in a five-person organization. It was obviously not a goal they could reach, but their slogan — "Act like five" — helped them see new possibilities for the way they conducted their day-to-day operations.

Visioning gets your hands off the rear-view mirror and onto the steering wheel, putting you in touch with future possibilities not just the past. Within the organization, four separate levels of visioning are required, one for each level of skilled behavior: senior executives, middle management, supervisors and individual contributors. For each, the reason for being is the same, but their perspective on how to paint themselves into the picture will vary with their assigned roles. The supervisor will imagine from the productivity and coaching role he or she has to play while keeping sighted on the organization's North Star. Middle managers will see their picture through the role of transforming executive initiative into meaningful plans, and creating a productive environment for work teams. Workers will see their personal work integrating effectively into the organization's master plan. These perspectives will all be different from the executive team's view. Even though their focus is on a different part of the mosaic it's the same picture. To be effective motivators, you must discover the differences, and keep asking employees the question, "What would it look like for you if it were just the way it should be?"

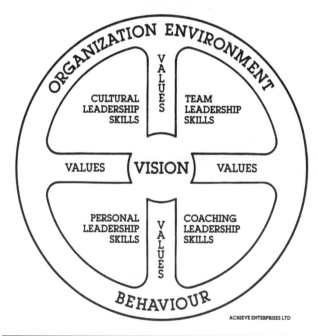

The vision-integrated-performance diagram on page 101 identifies how people at all four levels of your organization can get their hands onto the steering wheel. When visioning, it's just you, centered in the "I" of your hurricane, imagining how to make possible futures into realities. Try it.

LEADER PROFILE

Napoleon

Napoleon Bonaparte rose to prominence during the confusion and disorder of the French Revolution. At the time, France was being attacked by foreign armies on all sides, and plagued by internal power struggles. The populace was deeply divided. Many people were driven by revolutionary fervor while a large number of French citizens from all social levels clung to their feudal traditions.

While attention is usually focused on Napoleon's battlefield success, his greatest accomplishment was to create a new order out of the chaos, and unify the French people behind a set of ideas that shrewdly combined the best of the old and new regimes. To signal his intent, Napoleon chose a former Royalist and a Jacobean revolutionary as his fellow consuls when he first gained power. He did not discard liberty, equality and fraternity — the watchwords of the revolution — but spoke more of splendor, comprehension and efficiency.

To give his countrymen a sense of a new direction, Napoleon consciously used the mental picture of ancient Rome. Appealing to their imaginations, he promised to make Paris greater and more splendid than was Rome in its glory. In each conquered territory, Napoleon introduced the decimal system for measurement and currency — a symbol to these people that their world was changing, but as a counter to the revolutionary atmosphere, it also created a theme of reason, logic and order.

Wherever possible, Napoleon tried to unify warring factions within French society, in order to free up energy for other causes. The Revolution attacked the church as well as the French aristocracy and religious strife was rampant when Napoleon rose to power. He settled the issue in a manner that was in keeping with his values. Napoleon declared complete religious equality for Catholics, Protestants and other faiths. He called a council of Jewish rabbis and had his soldiers knock down the walls of Jewish ghettos as a symbol of new freedoms.

You could see his policy of combining the best of the old and new orders even in the way he handled military matters. The French army was deemed by many to be the best in Europe before the Revolution. To make it better still, Napoleon retained the skilled professionals — such as engineers and artillery experts — but got rid of mercenaries. He converted the army into a democratic institution. Napoleon declared to his troops that a field marshal's baton was tucked into every soldier's knapsack, a powerful signal to people conditioned to accept personal limits on their careers as dictated by the class system. He promoted those showing ability and, as a result, attracted many brilliant young officers and developed a body of dedicated well-motivated soldiers who were willing to make great sacrifices.

_____ *LEADER PROFILE* _____

Values
- splendor, comprehension and efficiency
- the belief that the ruler should be subject to the will of the people
- humanity versus despotism and rule by divine right

Vision
- surpassing the glory and might of ancient Rome

Signals:
- choosing a former Royalist and a Jacobean revolutionary as consuls
- declaring that there was a marshal's baton in every soldier's knapsack
- introducing the decimal system in conquered territories

Appropriate Leader Response to Challenge
- tearing down the walls of the Jewish ghettos
- blocking appointments and promotion of the old aristocracy unless the incumbent demonstrated ability

---

Part Two

Implementation Strategies

4

Signaling Scrimmages

Scrimmage: (a) messy, undisciplined tussle, (b) team members playing against each other in order to practice in close-to-real-game situations.

If this book advocated a new management technique there would be a comprehensive implementation plan. It doesn't, so there isn't. Offered instead, are low-risk experiments that you can toy with, off the playing field as it were, until you believe they have strategic relevance and feel sufficiently skilled to use them in the game of enterprise.

You've entertained the notion of vision and values, and hopefully targeted a few possibilities. Now it's time to discover how to properly apply a catalytic charge that will release the vast quantities of energy stored within your organization.

Most executives that I work with have been pleasantly surprised to discover how simple signaling skills are to apply once vision and values have been defined. Results can be dramatic. For this task, don't look outside of your normal work. Get out your day planner and review your existing itinerary. Each activity, every meeting with your staff, separately or in groups, provides an opportunity to send signals.

The trained manager in you may be predisposed to postpone beginning the activity of signal-sending while you perfect your vision and values, but energy comes only from action and the involvement of other people. Perfection may have its place in the turbulence, but it's not required or desired in your "I."

Where possible during this experiment, avoid initiating personal actions that do not complement what you are trying to communicate. Stay focused on your vision and values at all times. Don't make mechanical responses without first making a quick trip to your center. Practice your signaling skills with low-risk experiments where you can easily see results and needn't be too concerned about outcomes.

Purpose of Signaling

Signaling makes corporate vision clear but leaves the means of moving toward it open (within the boundaries of your declared set of core values) so that employees will be encouraged to innovate and become self-activated. In other words, signaling lets people know, through a set of consistent signals sent during normal day-to-day affairs, where the organization is headed, and what it believes in. When you communicate what you want without specifically telling, the leadership skills of subordinates have a greater chance to evolve, and more catalytic agents will become available to the organization.

Your First Day

Signals encompass action and visibility: the more the better. However, visibility at the start need not be a major issue. It can be increased as your confidence develops. But action must be present from the beginning.

I present scrimmages for a variety of values. Many will not apply to your organization but consider each and experiment with what seems to fit. I've known executives who tried to inject values into their organizations when they learned of another company's success. "That's us. That's what we have to do," was a usual response. It's OK to experiment with other people's experience but don't try to integrate a foreign concept until you are sure it fits. Just like the human body, organizations tend to reject foreign intrusions.

The Scrimmages

Customer Service

For Senior Executives: Visit your order desk and listen to your representative handling customer calls. Ask for his or her opinion about the level of service being provided. Ensure that no sense of judgments being made exists. This is a tough assignment. Initially, the order desk staff will assume you are there as a judging manager rather than as a leader who is trying to create energy. Remember, Archie Bunker didn't believe that he offended minorities — that's what made him so funny. Don't make assumptions. Make sure employees understand your intent.

Example: The chief executive of an insurance company was concerned because of a growing weight of evidence that suggested his firm had a serious problem with customer service. His first response was to consider training the staff, but first he decided to spend a morning in the customer service department. He advised the service staff in an informal way that because their work was so important, he wanted to find out exactly how they did things. The morale of service employees, and the quality of service being provided changed dramatically from that day forward. WHY? Because the leader demonstrated visible concern and personal support to the service function. He kept the momentum going by getting his service department managers to run regular skill practice for the staff. (The CEO kicked off the first training sessions personally.)

The training he selected did not deal with abstract ideas like the value of good customer service; rather, it focused on real-life issues such as answering the telephone by the third ring, and showing genuine concern for customers and their problems.

Comments: After you sent the service signal, did managers inquire as to why you visited the order desk? Did any action take place? How did service representatives respond to your interest in the level of service being provided? Do they now understand how service fits into your values? You won't likely be successful at creating a service improvement with one signal. Go back to your day planner. Imagine how you'd like your employees to behave with customers, then find a way to visibly model that behavior yourself. With a little imagination almost every action you take can be put to use. For instance, when speaking with his staff, one airline executive always makes a point of referring to customers as a primary asset, while referring to his fleet of aircraft as equipment.

For Managers: Tell your staff that you want to become more aware of clients' needs and that you intend to pay a personal visit to selected key customers in order to invite their feedback on your organization's service. Ask your staff to predict what you will hear. Also, explain to employees who have no external contacts that "customer" also means internal people for whom employees provide service. Staff groups too, have line customers. Place blank wall charts at each work station and ask staff to identify their "internal" customers.

Example: The owner of a sport clothing wholesale firm asked his sales people to identify the key market challenges and the personal win factors facing each of his company's best customers. He then visited each customer. Everyone was surprised to learn that less than 50 percent of the responses gathered by the boss showed any correlation to the predictions. From then on, more time was spent by sales reps making sure that they really knew the business of their key customers. Everyone in the company soon developed a "need to know" mindset when it came to key customers.

Comments: Involve people in your quest. Let them see that your signal of service really matters to you. You shouldn't interrupt your schedule or theirs. You want service to become part of everything they do, not just an item to be discussed at meetings. If people raise issues about your upcoming visits such as a customer's unrealistic delivery expectations, ask staff members, "Is it important to try to meet even an unrealistic customer's demands?" or "What internal changes would be required to make the impossible attainable?"

When you return from your visit, make a point of passing on what you learned. Give recognition for things done well. Explain the client's needs in human terms and bring them to life for your staff. Dialogue about your visit will have more impact than the figures in your numerical customer service index. Compare your group's prediction with what actually happened.

For Senior Executives: Conduct an after-hours management meeting in a retail outlet that markets your product, or a location where your services are used by consumers. Ask people to share their observations and feelings with you.

Example: An executive from a hardware chain moved his quarterly meeting to a neighborhood retail outlet. Prior to starting the meeting, the management team had a chance to informally mingle with the store's staff over coffee. The response was enthusiastic from employees who were delighted to see their leaders, and managers commented that issues seemed more relevant with increased personal contact. Now the executive team travels to a different store every other quarter.

Comments: Make sure not to develop a state visit mentality. Acting like royalty does not produce much energy. Remind your management team that they are there to send signals, not engage in "NOW HEAR THIS" messages or management snooping.

For Managers: During one-on-one discussions with staff members, ask what specific feedback they have heard from their customers in the last few weeks.

Example: A sales manager from a computer service company made regular telephone calls to his salespeople asking what suggestions they had heard recently from customers about the level of service being provided. He made a point of getting back to the customers who were identified personally, to let them know their suggestions had been heard. He also advised them what action was being taken or provided an explanation of why resolution was not possible.

Comments: Before an organization can "live for its customers," as many employees as possible must begin wondering what their customers are thinking. You signal your interest more by what you do with answers than you do by asking the questions.

For Managers: Provide etiquette training for telephone receptionists.

Example: An administration manager from a chemical company conducted a study that indicated his customers contacted the firm eighteen times by telephone for every face-to-face visit with an employee. Fortunes had been spent to ensure that their lobby was impressive and that field sales people were hired and trained to leave a good impression with customers. But telephone receptionists (with an 18:1 customer contact ratio) were left to their own devices. After the training program, telephone receptionists were aware of how critical their contributions were in the development of repeat business. Training helped, but the signal that the manager provided by introducing and supporting the training was the key.

Comments: Don't issue a memo. Take the opportunity to personally speak to employees, and explain that you will be taking training along with them *because customers are important.*

For Senior Executives: Get rid of policies that create barriers to the provision of good service. A usable definition of bureaucracy is any organization that determines policy based on internal criteria rather than on the needs of customers.

Example: When the chairman of Marks & Spencer was first appointed, he went on a sabbatical to hunt down and eliminate unnecessary paperwork. To signal the importance he placed on this drive, each time he identified regulations that could be eliminated he held a burning ceremony in front of Marks & Spencer staff. An old sacred cow policy that required several forms to be completed and attached as proof of purchase every time a customer wanted to return an item, was difficult to kill. The chairman suggested that customers should be allowed to bring products back without the need for documentation. The chairman's managers were convinced that such a policy would invite the entire United Kingdom to dump junk on the doorstep of Marks & Spencer. It turned out to be a classic case of an untested hypothesis. The chairman overruled the dissenters and imposed a new returns policy. Very few customers abused the system. The market, however, received a clear signal that Marks & Spencer trusted its customers, and the chairman saved massive costs by eliminating unnecessary paperwork. The paper elimination crusade excessed over five thousand jobs and Marks & Spencer had to implement a hiring freeze.

Comments: Don't be afraid to create events or use ceremony to make your point. People pay attention to show biz and will "get the picture" when it is used effectively.

For Managers: Seek out and retell your organization's legendary stories of performances that supported service. If you're from a new organization, search for industry stories that annoint service heroes.

Example: The senior manager of a government auditing team created a "best practices" award. Auditors were asked to look for groups of people doing a great job. These employees were invited to attend informal luncheons where they were asked to tell their story to managers from other departments. Managers in the audience then had a chance to ask questions. The end result was that managers learned and employees felt recognized. The managers then returned to their work teams armed with new stories to tell about successful innovation. The auditors enjoyed having something positive to contribute.

Comments: Consider calling retired employees and asking them to help you create a service hall of fame. Every organization has its Davy Crocketts — find them and tell their stories.

SCRIMMAGE: To signal a commitment to service

Pitfalls and Traps
- focusing on a specific customer with a problem and not following through to make sure that the problem won't happen to other customers
- not following up on or recognizing new initiatives that happen as a result of your signals
- others from your organization:

_____

_____

_____

_____

_____

_____

_____

_____

Action: Take your day planner. Circle the occasions on which you'll be meeting with your staff. Prepare a list of actions you could take to reinforce through your personal behavior how deeply you value service.

_____

_____

_____

_____

_____

_____

Self-Evaluation
What signals have I sent?

_____

_____

_____

_____

_____

What responses did I notice?

_____

_____

_____

_____

_____

What should I change or reinforce?

_____

_____

_____

_____

_____

We Value Our People

For Managers: Managers make repetitive or mundane tasks come alive by injecting energy. I remember an executive who told me that he liked the idea of signaling but couldn't find any time to participate. "I'm inundated with management responsibilities. For instance," he said, "tomorrow I spend the evening handing out length-of-service pins to employees. At times, I think it's a waste of time, but it's tradition around here."

Example: With a little prompting from his CEO to find a way to signal the value of people, he decided that rather than just hand out service pins, he would ask groups of recipients to come to his office for informal meetings. Over coffee he initiated a candid discussion with them about the organization's core values. He asked questions like, "Based on the experience of fifteen-year veterans, what do we do well around here? What are some of the dumbest things we do?"

Comments: If you have correctly identified a meaningful core value and have remained centered on your vision so that your signals are consistent, results will be noticeable; there will be an increase in energy and lots of enthusiasm.

For Senior Executives: Eliminate executive dining rooms and parking spaces. Encourage senior officers to mingle with their staff as frequently as possible. Set the example yourself to signal that you want to break down barriers between staff levels.

Examples: A manufacturing company removed small tables from its cafeteria and replaced them with large circular tables that sat ten people. Now, executives, marketers, clerks and operators can meet spontaneously. They have increased their awareness of and empathy with others, which means that jobs flow more smoothly and there is less counterproductive conflict.

An automotive company that sponsors an in-house slow-pitch baseball league enforces a rule that not more than three players from one department can play on the same team.

Comments: Many productive and innovative ideas come from chance meetings in lunch rooms, after hours, or in hallways. Make sure that your people have ample opportunity to contact each other informally.

For Senior Executives: Declare a Name Tag Day where employees from all levels will be actively encouraged (by the example of senior managers) to talk to each other on a first-name basis...

Example: A packaged food plant had a serious labor problem. A Name Tag Day was introduced and managers, labor leaders and workers were encouraged to spend the day talking to one another. It broke the ice and helped executives signal their desire to get back in touch. Now name tags are worn every day and executives, managers, and employees alike are recognizable as they walk through the plant or office.

Comments: Name tags won't have much impact on your personal secretary. She probably already knows more about you than you care to imagine. Make yourself visible to the whole team on this one. Wander around to different locations; address people by their first name and invite them to do the same with you. Remember to listen naively, and seize every opportunity to promote your values and vision.

For Managers: Reward perfect attendance with prizes.

Example: A telecommunications manufacturing plant in Mississippi holds a Bingo every morning. The general manager calls out a number over the company PA system. Employees must be present to record their number. One late day or absence and they miss the shot at the month's prize. One prize each month improved absenteeism and tardiness by 20 percent and everyone had fun besides.

Comments: People are important. Therefore, perfect attendance is a very legitimate activity to celebrate. And it's an opportunity to put some fun into the workplace. It can send a powerful signal as well. If putting on a chef's hat and wheeling lunch in on a trolley is not "you," find something else and take action to reward someone's performance.

It's important to recognize the specific behavior and not offer platitudes like "You guys are the greatest." A little guide to giving good feedback that I have found effective is "When you (*describe the specific behavior*), I felt (*declare your own feelings*)." If the observation is a negative, don't leave it there. You can add "Perhaps if you (*describe an alternate behavior*), it might (*declare possible consequences of the alternate behavior*).

For Managers and Supervisors: Ask machine operators to help during the selection of new equipment. Give them a say along with engineers and other specialists who are usually involved in such decision-making processes.

Example: A Pacific northwest manufacturer asked painters to take part in the design of a new paint shop. They suggested that the product be hung on paint racks a different way so that one complete step could be removed from the assembly process. At a national trade show, this company was the only one in its industry that didn't have to raise its prices (increased market power was made possible because of a painter's idea). The firm's sales increased by 28 percent that year.

Comments: Involving the staff who use equipment in decision-making will speed up effective implementation because potential problems can be solved early in the process.

For Supervisors: Provide employees with highly visible, pre-gummed UNSAFE stickers and explain that each person can use them on his own initiative wherever they find a safety problem. It's a great way to identify hazards and provides employees with a safe, uncomplicated vehicle through which they can communicate with superiors.

Example: A machine-shop superintendent was concerned about the time lost during the identification of unsafe equipment. Shop stewards, managers and workers were all involved. After stickers were introduced, maintenance staff acted to rectify unsafe situations without any other involvement. Management and labor got involved only when initial attempts at resolution failed.

Comments: Make sure that action is taken immediately when stickers are placed. (If no action is possible, let everyone know why.) Remember that your response to employees' placing of stickers is the most important part of your signal.

SCRIMMAGE: To signal how much you value people

Pitfalls and Traps
- Make sure you don't let a "concern for people" value cause supervisors and managers to avoid making hard performance decisions.
- Watch out for recognizing only management. Remember they're not the ones who do the real work.
- The first time around, some skepticism is to be expected; don't assume the signal wasn't appreciated even if initial responses were negative.
- Others from your organization;

_____
_____
_____
_____
_____

Action: Take out your day planner; list the scheduled activities that you can use to signal how deeply you value people.

_____
_____
_____
_____
_____

Self-Evaluation
What signals have I sent?

_____
_____
_____
_____
_____

_____

What responses did I notice?

_____

_____

_____

_____

_____

What should I change or reinforce?

_____

_____

_____

_____

_____

Quality

For Managers: Conduct frequent quality discussions and meetings at front-line locations where employees can see your concern first-hand.

Example: A plant manager from a paper products manufacturer with a serious quality problem, adopted the visible discussion approach to signal his commitment to quality. He experienced little improvement initially. Shoddy quality performance had placed his organization at the bottom of their industry's competitive heap and the job of every employee was in jeopardy if the situation wasn't turned around. The plant manager met with superintendents and shop foremen at different plant locations each day so that people could see *all* the company's defects. To enhance his signal of an uncompromising commitment to the quality issue, he was never late and he didn't let anything cause a rescheduling of meetings. Even when paged to take a call from the president, he would not leave until his quality meeting was completed. It took six months and more than a hundred meetings before significant improvement started to take place. In the following two and a half years, however, defects at the plant were cut by 75 percent and in many lines quality was considered to be number one in the industry.

Comments: Some signals will have significant impact right from the start. Others take weeks or months to permeate the organization and "unfreeze" the status quo.

For Managers: Give quality complaints broad circulation and ensure that concern is expressed vividly.

Example: The general manager of a textile company held weekly updates to review how quality problems were being dealt with. He took special pains to isolate problems that were not being solved satisfactorily by posting in red the number of weeks since the problem had been first identified.

Comments: Be consistent in your expressed concern for quality, and tenaciously follow through to ensure resolution. People must regularly get an uncompromised, powerful message about your obsession with quality.

For Middle Managers: Take production supervisors to outlets where your product or service is purchased or used.

Example: A leading food processor held a series of visits to grocery retail outlets for their production people. Many of the male employees had not visited a supermarket in years. It was a revelation for them to talk with consumers who bought their product, and the products of competitors. A recently introduced packaging redesign, which was held in very low esteem at the plant, was quickly accepted once the machine operators saw how it was winning the attention of consumers.

Comments: When you make a visit, make sure that participants have a specific task assigned, asking buyers about their perception of quality, for instance. Make sure to follow through with a meaningful de-briefing exercise and act on as many suggestions as you can.

For Managers: Look for opportunities to be seen dramatically living out your quality obsession. For example, ceremonially scrap product that does not live up to standards.

Example: An aircraft assembly manager made his quality concerns visible by leaving rejects in a prominent spot and posting a sign that read, "Not up to our standards."

Comments: Employees accustomed to their organization's opting for profits over quality will recognize that you are signaling commitment only when you put your money where your mouth is.

For Managers: Look for quality improvements and celebrate with as much fanfare as you can muster once you discover them.

Example: A California-based pharmaceutical CEO enjoys gourmet cooking. Every month, to recognize quality contributions, he invites recognized performers to his home where he prepares a fabulous meal. An interesting aspect of these events is that several vice-presidents also attend — to serve the food.

Comments: One of the advantages in involving junior

managers during the sending of your signal is that they also have a chance to get the message and to follow your lead.

For Managers: Make an event out of developing a quality slogan.

Example: A supermarket produce manager introduced a contest for all her employees. The quality slogan that was selected as most appropriate by all the produce employees would win a dinner for two. She made sure that lots of honorable mention T-shirts with the slogan "Let's keep ahead of the competition," were handed out along with the winning prize. The chain's performance audit team noted that her store's produce display was far superior to that of the nearest challenger.

Comments: Involve staff in selecting the winner. Issue everyone who makes a suggestion with some form of recognition. One enterprising slogan I came across read, "Contacts can help managers see quality more clearly."

SCRIMMAGE: To support quality

Pitfalls and Traps
- Employees may see your drive for quality as an opportunity to slack off on productivity.
- Don't expect short-term payoff. Initially you may have to scrap more product than you bargained for. But research shows that once workers develop a quality mindset, it doesn't cost, it pays.
- Don't accept the argument that quality always costs. More money could be spent to make a Cadillac out of a Honda, but doing well what you sign up to do is the essence of quality.

Others from your organization:

_____
_____
_____
_____
_____

Action: Look for activities that you can use to signal a deep personal commitment to quality.

_____
_____
_____
_____
_____

Self-Evaluation
What signals have I sent?

_____
_____
_____
_____
_____

What response did I notice?

_____
_____
_____
_____

What should I change or reinforce?

_____
_____
_____
_____
_____

Innovation

For Senior Executives: Make sure that managers and employees make time to search for new ideas and better ways of doing things.

Example: A hydro-electric executive invited managers to suggest how much engineering time should be allocated to research. The response was 10 percent of each workday, with an employee committee to allocate the time. The executive felt that their proposed system was too cumbersome but decided to let his team find that out themselves rather than signal any lack of trust on his part. Eventually, management and the engineers changed the suggested time to 5 percent on average. The research project went on to produce exceptional results, perhaps because all those involved had a feeling of ownership and wanted to make the experiments work.

Comments: Implementation is just as important if not more so than planning and deciding. Take a lesson from the Japanese and take time to work through implementation issues.

For Senior Executives: Visit employees whose attempts at innovation have failed. Discuss your feelings about the importance of new ideas and ask how the organization might learn from their effort.

Example: The parts department manager of an automobile service centre had a clerk working for him who was taking computer programming at night school. On his own time, the clerk designed a system for keeping customer service records. The innovation was not sophisticated enough to capture all the required data. However, the parts manager discussed the supposed failure with his employee and, after developing an understanding of the clerk's intent, decided that mechanized customer service records were a good idea. A consultant was subsequently hired to build a program and the clerk was assigned as the primary internal resource for the project.

Comments: The company got their system, the employee felt recognized and as well, learned from the consultant.

For Senior Executives: Visit a research team and let them know, without interfering, how important their efforts are.

Example: The CEO of a company seriously outpaced by its competition for new ideas decided to spend an entire day with the staff of a key research project. Not able to understand the technical difficulties involved, he paid attention to subjects he could relate to and soon uncovered a thicket of bureaucratic obstacles that were holding up the project, and causing the research team to suffer low self-esteem. Once obstacles were cleared, the research team's performance improved dramatically.

Comment: Learn to listen naively. You're there to energize.

SCRIMMAGE: To signal a commitment to innovation

Pitfalls and traps

- Don't expect every initiative to succeed. Make sure you minimize the magnitude of risk by breaking the project up into bite-sized chunks.

- Put a stop on innovations that are not compatible with your values or vision.

- Don't focus exclusively on big projects. Minor innovations can be profitable and afford you more frequent opportunities to recognize performance.

- Make sure that you orchestrate to involve the creativity of *all* employees.

- One of the hardest aspects of an executive's job is allowing employees to follow through on their ideas EVEN IF THE IDEAS ARE NOT PERFECT. You must let people learn by their mistakes. Search for low-risk opportunities for them to test their wings.

- Manage down the size of risk by experimenting as you go. Don't design the master plan on paper. TEST, TEST, TEST as you go.

Others from your organization:

_____

_____

_____

_____

_____

Action: Identify the scheduled activities that you can use to signal your commitment to innovation.

_____

_____

_____

_____

_____

Self-Evaluation
What signals have I sent?

_____
_____
_____
_____
_____
_____

What response did I notice?

_____
_____
_____
_____
_____
_____

What should I change or reinforce?

_____
_____
_____
_____
_____
_____

Vision

When you signal a value that is right for your organization — one that a critical mass of people have real feelings for — you'll know because of the amount of energy that will be unlocked. Vision, unlike values, does not already exist, it must be created. No foolproof way exists to check on the choice you have made for vision. The best you can do is have it feel right. The initial response of your staff to vision may not be positive, but if you have made a reasonable choice, in time you will notice employees becoming more focused. All the energy that your core values create will start moving in the same direction.

Don't make any grand announcements until you are ready. Signal your vision again and again, until a critical mass of employees get it. And then keep on signaling by stepping up the fanfare.

Reason for Being

For Managers: Place priorities on scheduled activities that are congruent with your reason for being; cut back the time spent on other things.

Example: A hospital had adopted a reason for being of earning the respect of the community but initially they made little headway. The administrator kept at it by making sure that his management team's meeting agenda allowed abundant time for any items that contributed to the reason for being. He kept non-compatible items off the agenda whenever possible. Within three months, his focus permeated beyond departmental heads and others started to "get the picture."

Comments: People pay attention to whatever you spend your time doing. Visibly reinforce only what is relevant to your reason for being. As a leader, you should not water down your obsession. Delegate non-related tasks, or do them at times when there are no observers.

For Senior Executives: Make a "no going back" gesture.

Example: A manufacturing company executive publicly declared, as part of the corporation's annual report, his intent to radically change the company's management style. Proposed action included decentralization and the assignment of more autonomy for people. The strategy was re-confirmed, as part of the report, by each vice-president (whose picture appeared above his or her comments). There could be no going back. Shareholders, employees, suppliers, the union, and the board of directors "got the picture."

Comments: To visibly demonstrate the power of your reason for being, the equivalent of burning your boats, is an effective strategy.

For Managers: Eliminate dysfunction (anything that inhibits movement toward your reason for being). Get rid of elements that don't fit in: fire senior and middle managers who aren't adapting; recognize those who are; check with the leader of your human resource department about your implementation of proposed changes, and encourage him or her to interact with line managers to plan whatever training will be needed.

Example: A telephone company asked a marginally performing vice-president who had displayed little interest in the company's reason for being to take early retirement or be fired. Up to that point senior officers, in the eyes of their subordinate managers, had appeared to be beyond any requirement to demonstrate personal performance. The signal was clear. Marginal performance was no longer good enough, even for those with position or tenure.

Comment: Make sure that other development options have been tried before you initiate separation discussions.

*SCRIMMAGE: Signaling your commitment to reason
for being*

Pitfalls and Traps

- All your words should paint a vivid mental picture of your preferred future. Don't be too detailed or overly technical.
- Make sure that the preferred future of senior managers is compatible with the organization's reason for being.
- Others from your organization:

_____
_____
_____
_____
_____
_____

ACTION: List the activities already planned for the next week that you can use to signal your reason for being.

_____
_____
_____
_____
_____
_____

Articulate a *reason for being* for yourself and family.

_____
_____
_____
_____
_____
_____

Self-Evaluation
What signals have I sent?

What response did I notice?

What do I need to change or reinforce?

Visioning

For organizations built on years of cold, hard rational thinking and a staid corporate culture, acceptance of the concept of visioning will not come easily. If you tell employees that you want them to try visioning, you'll get resistance. And they'll disappear until the new "fad" goes away. If, instead, you signal your desire to encourage the activity of visioning, and personally demonstrate how effective it can be, you'll get better results.

For Senior Executives: Begin your next board meeting by presenting next year's annual report as though results have already been successfully achieved. Then go back and isolate what is inhibiting, and contributing to, the possibility of the "ideal" happening. Declare your plans to capitalize on the contributing factors and look for ways to minimize the impact of inhibitors.

Example: An international land developer had the company's top thirty executives attend a three-day conference. To explain corporate direction, the president and vice-chairman presented a discussion entitled "Five Years from Now." They talked as though they had already arrived there and were looking back at five years of success. It was an inspirational way to discuss a five-year perspective without weighing people down with planning details that are bound to change because of unforeseen realities.

Comment: Long-range plans can be limiting — particularly in a business where opportunity can present itself at any time. Visioning provides a functional alternative. It's the marketer's "pro-forma."

For Supervisors: When taking on a new assignment, ask your manager to describe how he or she sees the situation one year from now (or less) if everything goes perfectly. Probe to gain a clear understanding, then develop your action plans to move toward your boss's vision.

Example: A supervisor of an engineering division was asked to relocate professionals to another floor. He was given, as part of his assignment, the task of drawing up a floor plan. Rather than design exclusively to meet his own objectives, the supervisor asked his boss to imagine that the move had already happened and to describe in detail what he saw happening. In the boss's visioning colleagues were gathering around each other's work stations to collaborate on a volume of exciting new projects. In the plan the supervisor allowed space to accommodate the "vision" of crowding around work stations and he won the wholehearted support of his boss the first time his layout was presented.

Comments: Asking people to engage in visioning — "seeing it" being successful — can provide valuable tips on what needs to be done to gain acceptance. Often, issues not consciously known to the person visioning are uncovered. That's the value of seeing rather than talking.

For Managers: At the beginning of your next meeting, ask participants to take five minutes to personally answer the following questions:
a) What are your realistic expectations for the outcome of today's meeting?
b) What do you hope won't happen?
c) What can you do to prevent (b) from happening?

Example: The manager of a telephone selling team asked each person to read out their personal expectations. (Question a). She documented common themes on a flip chart in front of the group. At the end of the meeting she then returned to the items listed on the flip chart and asked for comments on how well her people had met their own expectations. She asked participants to identify their rating for each expectation by raising fingers — 5 for "yes," expectation was met; 3, marginally met; and 1, not met at all.

Comments: Did the meeting run smoothly? Did people control their own behavior and take responsibility for getting results? If they did, congratulate them on a job well done. Later on, subtly investigate whether any of your managers open future meetings in a similar manner.

For Managers: When your employees approach you with a problem, stop them before they get too far into their explanations and ask them to describe what the situation would look like if it were not a problem. After they have completed this visioning exercise, ask what can be done to move toward this preferred future.

Example: Encourage employees to brainstorm ideas and make it clear you don't want an analytical report.

Comments: When excitement starts to build, signal through your behavior your approval of their process and get out of their way.

For Managers: When interacting on a performance issue, ask the person to imagine that he or she has corrected the problem and has already produced outstanding results. Discuss what success looks like.

Example: Isolate the key performance factors by noting the difference between what is and what could be. For each key factor, brainstorm to identify *inhibitors* that are blocking movement toward what could be. Brainstorm to discover *contributors* that will enhance movement toward what could be.

Comments: Develop an action plan to capitalize on contributors and minimize inhibitors. Establish mid-point target dates. (This process, called Force Field Analysis, was developed by Kurt Lewin.)

SCRIMMAGE: To signal the effectiveness of visioning

Pitfalls and Traps
- Visioning is used in the same way an accountant uses a pro-forma. Do not treat it like an objective that must be met.
- Make sure that everyone clearly understands the difference between what you are imagining and reality.
- Others from your organization:

_____
_____
_____
_____
_____
_____

Action: List the planned activities you can use to signal the effectiveness of visioning.

_____
_____
_____
_____
_____
_____

Self-Evaluation
What signals have I sent?

_____
_____
_____
_____
_____
_____

What response did I notice?

_____

_____

_____

_____

_____

_____

What should I change or reinforce?

_____

_____

_____

_____

_____

_____

Working with Your Staff

For Senior Executives: In your memos make a specific issue of qualifying your requests for information from subordinate managers by stating the maximum amount of time you want invested in the project. After two weeks, go to lower levels and see if anyone has picked up on your intent.

Examples: During my stint in the military, the camp commander noted on the margin of a memo that the barracks were showing peeled paint. That weekend, all passes were canceled and hundreds of military man-hours were spent painting the buildings. On Monday, it was discovered that a contract had already been signed with a civilian contractor to do the painting job. Guess what? The barracks received an unnecessary additional coat of paint.

One of my clients now places an A, B or C rating on all his requests to express the intensity of response that he expects.

Other executives have replaced memos, where possible,

with face-to-face communication or a telephone call so that intent can be clarified through feedback.

Comments: Ask subordinates if, in their opinion, there is less time being spent collecting data in response to management requests for information? Does less paperwork come across your desk? Are the memos you receive simple and brief? If they are, put a winner's seal on the good examples and circulate them.

For Managers: Ask your secretary to describe her idea of a Utopian boss/subordinate relationship. What would it be like if she were exquisitely organized, with access to everything she needed. What would you have to alter to become a perfect boss? Ask her to guess what you would write about her strengths and weaknesses. In fairness, you should guess how she would rate your strengths and weaknesses as well.

Prepare a list of points you agree on and let go of erroneous assumptions. Devise action plans to deal with weaknesses on both sides.

Example: The administrative assistant of a successful land developer has been working for the president since the company's incorporation. It had been a perfect match for years but, because of rampant growth, both she and her boss had lost sight of each other's increasing workload. After a doctor's diagnosis of "excessive stress," they sat down and talked for an entire uninterrupted day. Many new realities were uncovered and the pair re-negotiated their expectations.

Comments: Don't wait for incidents before you invest time talking to your administrative support staff. They are an integral part of your performance team and need to get the signal that you care. Don't let familiarity breed contempt.

SCRIMMAGE: To support working with your staff

Pitfalls and Traps
Talking about things rather than doing something is a common failing of managers when dealing with support staff. In this case, the role of "doing" is yours, not theirs.

Others from your organization:

_____
_____
_____
_____
_____
_____

Actions: With support staff, ask for and list what you can do to make their job easier.

_____
_____
_____
_____
_____
_____

Did your staff agree with your ideas or offer other suggestions?

_____
_____
_____
_____
_____
_____

What I will do to follow through with action?

_____
_____
_____

Canceling Unwanted Signals

Any signal that is sent, intentionally or otherwise, remains in existence until deliberately stamped out by someone in authority. In the meantime, they act as barriers to energy flow. No matter how well you remain centered personally, your organization will undoubtedly send mixed signals.

Many organizations are hampered by signals about maintaining tight controls that were spawned during the recession. Every organization has a few energy destroyers rattling around preventing initiative and causing confusion. Common problem areas are:

- rules about the number of levels required to approve expenditures. They may have made sense in response to the credit crunch of recession, but now that you have to move quickly, what signal are you sending to front line people?

- managers who overdo a "need to know." If your people are struggling to become more competitive, the signal they get will be that times aren't changing. We still have to waste time going through the same old "the boss needs to know" routines.

- unintentional anti-innovation signaling: You won't get employees to experiment with becoming innovative if you take a follow-the-party-line stance. Cancel this signal.

- the good news syndrome: How can you respond quickly in a fast-changing marketplace if you don't have good information? You need to signal that you won't shoot messengers bearing bad news.

- brownie points issued for being a button-down bureaucrat: Every executive would like to think that he or she rewards results not style, but research suggests that many employees get recognized for apple-polishing and upward sensitivity.
- save the dimes/forget the dollars: Counting-paperclips behavior from a boss when large challenges or opportunities exist is demoralizing and it destroys energy.
- treating people like cogs in the machine: People tend to live up (or down) to the expectations that you have of them. Altering a culture with low executive expectations is an impossible task.

For All Managers: Ask people at all levels (and tell them you're asking the same question at all levels): What are some of the dumbest things we do around here?

For All Managers: To help overcome a sense of "we are looking for you to screw up," ask your audit team to conduct a best practices audit, looking for sections that are doing things extremely well. Publish a list of excellent practices, then hold a session where your "heroes" are recognized for what they have done (make sure their excellent behaviors are explicitly stated). Invite managers to interview the panel of winners to gain insight into how they accomplished their success.

SCRIMMAGE: To cancel unwanted signals

Pitfalls and Traps
Don't expect to finish the job the first day. Keep the lines of communication open on a continuing basis. Many of these energy-destroyers have become so much a part of the organization's culture that despite their high frustration

factor, they are hard to spot. You hope there won't be any unwanted signals sent in the future but....

Action: Take out your day planner and list the scheduled activities you can use to find and eradicate unwanted signals.

_____

_____

_____

_____

_____

_____

What signals did I send?

_____

_____

_____

_____

_____

What did I do to keep the lines of communication open?

_____

_____

_____

_____

_____

Signaling Your Primary Strategies

You can — and already do — send signals that relate to management goals and objectives. Your actions determine what will be brought to the foreground of your staff's perception. If you complain about irrelevant items like how many paperclips are being wasted, you will draw non-productive issues to the fore. But if you remain centered in spite of the turbulence (focused on vision and aware of core values) you will naturally begin to dwell on issues that have the potential for real impact.

Example: An important part of one real estate manager's strategy was to cut overheads. Rather than let people go he found reports that were costly to prepare. Many were perceived to be sacred cows in the organization. He announced that, as an experiment, he wanted to do without the reports for a year, just to see if they were really needed.

Comments: By eliminating reports that were previously perceived as untouchable, he opened the door to the re-evaluation of all practices. Less than 5 percent of most executives' time is spent engaged in making a visible, direct contribution to their organization's primary strategy. And, upon close inspection, whatever time is spent, produces little in the way of bottom-line results. Many senior executives have lost sight of the impact that their mundane actions have on subordinates.

SCRIMMAGE: To signal aspects of your primary strategy

Pitfalls and Traps
Is the strategy you selected getting increased airtime from your manager? Is anything happening? Annoint heroes when you notice their reacting appropriately. Be vocal and specific.

Action: Take an existing primary strategy and determine what you need from your subordinate managers to make it happen. Select an action that will signal to everyone (without saying it) that you consider this specific issue important and expect results. Execute your signal via personal action.

What signals did I send?

_____
_____
_____
_____
_____

What response did I notice?

_____
_____
_____
_____
_____

What should I change or reinforce?

_____
_____
_____
_____
_____

Eventually, as your confidence in signaling increases, you will alter the way you plan your day in order that more time can be spent being visible to your staff. In a week or two, there will be a real difference in how others perceive your visibility. Imagine visible actions that may not fit into your present schedule, but might be suitable for inclusion in future plans.

Florence Nightingale

It was not until the age of thirty-two, after a long battle with herself and her family, that Florence Nightingale settled on a career of nursing. In 1852, nurses were characterized as tipsy, unprofessional and on a par with prostitutes. Health care was in a deplorable state. Patients died with alarming frequency from diseases caught during their stay in hospital. The relevance of proper sanitary conditions was just beginning to be understood.

She envisioned a future where the health-care system would be governed by strict professional standards, where both doctors and nurses would provide care as well as contribute to improvements in the patient's overall health. Nurses, she believed, should always be self-controlled regardless of what might happen around them. They should be selfless, and professional in every way.

She believed strongly in contributing to the dignity of people. Nurses were the most obvious beneficiaries of her reasoning, but patients benefitted as well. The signals she sent were so pervasive that the status of her patients — Britain's soldiers and sailors — also rose following the Crimean War. Her entire Crimean experience contained many messages that were heard by the general public. Her every act signaled her values and visions. It is said that upon her arrival at the hospital in Scutari, a rat appeared in the cramped nurses' quarters. Women screamed and ran, but Miss Nightingale intervened to kill the rat with her shoe, again signaling that she expected rational behavior from her staff at all times.

For months after arriving at Scutari, doctors refused to allow Florence's nurses to attend patients. She maintained a controlled and reserved professional attitude throughout the conflict, always behaving consistently with her view of how nurses should act.

There were a number of upper middle class "ladies" assigned to her nursing staff. Although they had social con-

147

nections that would have helped Forence's cause, the ladies were unwilling to personally provide the kind of patient care Miss Nightingale called for. She sent them packing.

Fame spread rapidly after her contribution to the Crimean War. The "Lady of the Lamp" became known all over the world. Florence's war experiences were only part of her long battle to make changes to the health-care system. As a result of her leadership, the role of nurses changed for all time. Despite the slow pace of improvements, she maintained a firm belief that progress was being made. Her behavior was so exemplary of her values and vision that she set a standard for nursing behavior that is in use to this day.

An able administrator, she was also noted for her ability to tear the essentials out of the most lengthy report. In 1861, the U.S. War Office used her work as a model for field hospitals and nursing training.

Values
- the dignity of patients and staff
- a caring health system
- persistence in the face of obstacles

Vision
- She envisaged a health-care system run with strict professional standards for both doctors and nurses.
- She maintained her vision despite constant obstacles that had to be overcome.

Signals
- the care she herself provided to patients
- killing the rat instead of fleeing
- entering the much-maligned nursing profession in the first place

Appropriate Leader Response to Challenge
- maintaining professional standards and waiting patiently at Scutari for permission to attend patients
- dismissing society ladies who were not prepared to get personally involved in the provision of proper care

5

Challenge and the Appropriate Response: Playing the Game — to Win

Signaling core values and vision in controlled experiments where you choose the conditions and have time to plan your moves ahead of time is one thing. Doing the same thing under pressure, in situations created by employees or the marketplace, is quite different, as different as scrimmages and the big game. To win the battle to make your values and vision come alive you must be visible to employees, both challenging and challenged.

Most new management programs spawned in the classroom ultimately fall by the wayside because, to employees, they appear academic, something apart from day-to-day reality, not part of the real work. And in a crisis, these doubting employees are usually proven correct. Managers under fire quickly put new theories aside and return to tried and tested methods. Creating corporate energy, however, can work because you develop it on the fly as an integral part of your job. And, because you live it all the more when challenged, employees will know it is real.

The lion's share of all functional innovation occurs in

the field, where ideas can be challenged in the cold, hard light of day, by real people. Products or services rarely succeed the way researchers or designers initially imagine them. Success more often happens the wrong way, in the wrong place or at the wrong time. High-performance organizations from this decade recognize this. They regularly force R&D and marketing people to mingle with the real world. The winners see effective R&D as an evolving set of scaled-down experiments where each small win or failure is useful in shaping eventual success.

If a new project consists only of paper plans, and testing doesn't begin until a finished prototype is ready for the field, implementation will more often than not be a nightmare. Senior managers have forgotten that the essence of scientific method is to collect data from experiments. The process is empirical and theory is formed on the back end of testing, not the other way round.

The principles involved in the scientific method also apply in creating corporate energy. The benefit of leaders being out in the field, aggressively challenging and inviting challenge, is that "mini learnings" result. Shifts toward improved performance evolve from a myriad of seemingly unrelated initiatives, unrelated, that is, to those trapped in the turbulence. For people who have learned to access their "I," the process can transform random and spontaneous challenge into energy for a focused strategic thrust, with potential for huge payoffs. But remember, employees stuck in the turbulence of day-to-day affairs may not "see" the logic of your action. You could well be a villain in their eyes — until results start to emerge.

Challenge

If you are constantly challenging employees to live values and vision and if you are signaling consistently your willingness to accept challenge, the excitement you unleash will encourage people at all levels to take part. But employees are going to have their own ideas about how to move toward the vision. As they begin to challenge and innovate, only unvarying support from senior management will keep the energy flowing and expanding during what is a period of high personal risk for them. If their opinions have not been asked for in years, they will be in unfamiliar waters.

One CEO decided he would overcome the recalcitrance of his organization and encourage innovation by presenting an award to employees who had accepted a challenge but failed in the endeavor. He asked his managers to supply names, intending to involve them in sending a signal that the organization valued challenge and innovation to the extent that they would be prepared to accept some failure. But his management team balked. In their minds it was wrong to celebrate failure, and their resistance put the CEO in an interesting position. The management team's response was, in itself, a challenge for which he had to find an appropriate response. The CEO overruled his team and went on to present his award, but not before explaining in great detail that what he was doing was based on the strength of his commitment to overcoming the organization's fear of trying new things. He wanted to develop an environment that encouraged people to challenge the traditional way of doing things.

Initial signals about your willingness to accept challenge can be planned in advance but, like the Sorcerer's Apprentice, be warned that you may discover there is more going on than you bargained for.

Examples: If everyone at a meeting agrees, ask your team to play the devil's advocate and challenge popular opinion on the subject under discussion.

Ask your team members to put themselves in the shoes of potential resisters who are not in the room, and enthusiastically present their views.

Ask employees to develop multiple solutions to problems and present the pros and cons of each.

For all Managers: Find ways to challenge employees to live the organization's values and vision.

Example: Convinced that the surest route to understanding something is having to explain it, the CEO of an east coast engineering firm challenges his people to discuss his company's values and vision with prospective employees. Once the applicants for any position have been short-listed they are asked to join a frank give-and-take session with a cross section of employees who explain what values and vision mean to their organization.

Comments: Having staff members verbalize their thoughts helps to remove values and vision from the theoretical level and sends a clear signal to both current and prospective employees.

> *SCRIMMAGE: To signal your eagerness to accept challenge*

Pitfalls and Traps
- You won't invite much challenge with words alone. Be assured that you will not always get the challenge you expect.
- To be effective, your signal needs to be received and understood by all levels of the organization.
- People may use challenge to play one-upmanship with each other by "shooting down" new ideas.
- Others from your organization:

_____
_____
_____
_____
_____
_____
_____

Action: Devise a situation that will encourage challenges to your values or vision from within the ranks of your organization. Let your people see you enthusiastically welcoming the challenge when it is received. Celebrate its occurrence.

_____
_____
_____
_____
_____
_____

Self-Evaluation
What signals have I sent?

_____
_____
_____
_____
_____

What responses did I notice?

_____
_____
_____
_____
_____

What needs to be changed or reinforced?

_____
_____
_____
_____

How can you visibly celebrate challenge when it occurs?

_____
_____

Encouraging people to take initiative will provoke challenges to your business plan, policies and procedures. Remember that these challenges will be attempts to question the barriers within your organization, barriers to energy.

Getting integrated support from all levels at the same time will require a great deal of creativity on your part. Many Quality Circle programs ultimately fail because middle managers were not really involved. They simply got bored with the process because there was no visible sign of real interest coming from senior management, and no consequences, pro or con, to encourage their personal involvement.

SCRIMMAGE: To welcome challenge to policy or strategy

Pitfalls and Traps
If you support the challenge, signals will be easy to send. Your signal will be tougher but no less important when you have to oppose the challenge.

Possibilities
People will learn to be more accepting of hard realities if they see you connect unpopular business discussions to the organization's values and vision.

Action: Look for anyone who identifies problems with policy. Visibly signal how much you value this challenge and see if the issue can be worked through to a successful conclusion.

Identify challenges to your business plan.

How will you signal challenges that you support?

And challenges you can not support:

Plan signals you can send to other levels of the organization that will promote recognition of how important the issue of challenge is:

The Appropriate Response

Management schools have taught us to respond to problems and challenges by solving or getting rid of them. "Don't let it impact the bottom line. Don't let anything happen that could negatively affect your business plan."

Many parents adopt a similar approach to raising their children. Of course rules are necessary to guide the young through their early years, but if rules are all that children get, they'll be in trouble when they find themselves in situations where the old rules don't apply. For example, when leaving home for college or work, they may not be equipped to make effective decisions and form rules of their own that suit the new environment. Whereas, if parents take time to explain the reasoning behind rules, and if rules are tied to the family's values as well as to the children's vision of their preferred future, the children, while still making mistakes, will at least have an understanding of where they are going and why.

An appropriate response to challenge, whether it is a business plan at work or rules at home, is any response that creates — rather than destroys — energy. Executives still have to make the tough business decisions. Your actions must fit with realities dictated by the marketplace. But you can get creative during tough times and find responses that will allow you to get the difficult jobs done while still remaining centered in your "I." The challenge is to find a response that further entrenches the values and vision in the minds of employees. Try testing your response with questions like "Before I do what I'd like, is my action in line with our values and vision, as well as with the business plan." Thinking it through will help you remain centered. Saying out loud how your action will connect with values and vision and explaining it in front of your people will not only signal your commitment, it will also reinforce how they should respond to their own challenges in the future.

There is not always a chance to plan your reactions to challenge ahead of time — which is precisely why employees will be energized when you respond appropriately. But you can prepare yourself in advance. Imagine potential challenges and examine your automatic responses. Remember, the standard of measurement of appropriateness is the amount of energy you create or destroy.

Common Challenges
• A customer insists that he or she has not been given what he or she contracted for on a large project.

Energy-destroying Response: Take the legal approach and attempt to prove that contractually the customer is wrong. Look at the mixed signals being sent to employees and customers if you've been signaling how much you value service.

A Better Response: Display genuine concern. Try to correct the situation in such a way that everyone sees that you do not expect any recurrence of the problem.

Your Approach:

_____
_____
_____
_____
_____
_____

• A radical change in your market forces you to permanently lay off one third of your workforce.

Energy-destroying Response: Stay in your office and delegate the firing to others. Keep everyone in the dark and make sure that all employees being let go are ordered off the site immediately.

A Better Response: A few years ago, a petrochemical company chose "respect for the individual" as one of its core values. Only one month after the selection, when everyone in the organization was just starting to get excited about living their values and vision, the bottom fell out of the oil market. The company had no choice but to let people go. It looked as though they'd have to let their values around respect for the individual go too. The roar of the turbulence must have been very loud, but they remained true to their "I," deciding to handle the layoffs in a way that demonstrated to the greatest degree possible the respect they had for people. Line managers were given skills-training on how the situation was to be handled, both in dealing with employees and with their own feelings on the subject. Then a private interview was conducted with every employee. Those who were staying were told what was happening and why, and what was being done for the others. Those who were being let go were also given background information explaining why it was happening. A special effort was made to help people survive. Separation payments were liberal. As a result, those who were released retained good feelings toward the organization, and the remaining team was not at all demoralized — quite the opposite in fact. The company's value statement was believed even after a major layoff. It had been tested under fire.

Your Response:

_____

_____

_____

_____

_____

_____

SCRIMMAGE: To practice the appropriate response

Pitfalls and Traps:
You often find yourself forced to choose between losing a battle and winning the war. The test of leadership is to stay focused on the long term even when forced to make short-term decisions. People need leadership more than ever during periods of turmoil. You can energize employees by showing them how the seeds of eventual victory can be found even during the agony of defeat.

• Others from your organization:

_____
_____
_____
_____
_____
_____

Action: Pick one or more challenges from the following list, or identify one that is frequently thrown at you. Plan a response that is appropriate with your values and vision.

• You lose a customer to the competition.

• You promote someone and another employee complains that he or she was better qualified.

• One of your direct reports has a personal crisis at home.

• Under new environmental laws your organization's standard practices leave you open to pollution charges.

• A recently acquired company has a markedly different "culture" from the rest of your organization.

• You discover misdirected competition between two divisions.

Identify what aspects of your values, vision and business plan could be affected by challenge.

_____
_____
_____
_____
_____
_____

Working with the opposite to what you really want will free your imagination. Select three responses to challenge that would be devastating to your organization's energy.

_____
_____
_____
_____
_____

Choose two responses that will maintain or create energy.

_____
_____
_____
_____
_____

Every organization has its mavericks — those who can be counted on to challenge almost everything you do. A Harvard article suggests that the health of an organization is inversely proportional to the size of the gap between the direction taken by executives and that taken by unofficial group leaders or mavericks.

Kurt Lewin developed a problem-solving process called force field analysis. Draw a line down the middle of a page and on one side list all the positive forces that drive your organization: incentive programs, loyalty, the need to meet a tight deadline, etc. The status quo exists because there are an equal number of negative or inhibiting forces on the other side of the line holding you back. If you add more drivers, you'll move forward for a while but more resisters are likely to appear, and you have no way of knowing what they will be. If, on the other hand, you concentrate on removing resisting forces, you have an excellent opportunity to successfully alter the status quo.

Dr. Ron Lippett, Professor Emeritus at Michigan State, and affectionately referred to as the grandfather of planned change, insists that resisters can become the organization's best allies. If you fight resisters, you lose; if you find a way to make use of their energy, you win. It's like judo. You use the resister's power to help you get where you want to go.

For too many organizations, organized labor has become a group maverick. Executives waste energy trying to fight them, or trying to add more driving forces. A better solution would be to welcome their challenges and respond in a way that draws their energy toward your "I."

> *SCRIMMAGE: To welcome challenge from the*
> *organization's mavericks*

Pitfalls and Traps:
What is appropriate to the situation will not always be congruent with values and vision. You may be asked to live with a paradox. Leaders can do it if they remain centered.

• Others from your organization:

_____

_____

_____

_____

_____

_____

Possibilities
Action: Signal to known mavericks within your organization that you welcome their challenge. When the next challenge presents itself, respond in a manner both visible and appropriate.

_____

_____
_____
_____
_____
_____

_____

What activities can you design to get your mavericks to challenge you?

_____

_____
_____

_____

_____

What will your responses be?

_____

_____
_____
_____

_____

The feedback I get from executive teams that I work with shows that the same process is particularly helpful in dealing with home or family situations.

Action: Pick a challenge to your own individual values or vision that you face in your personal life. Plan an appropriate response.

_____

_____
_____
_____
_____
_____

_____

Indicate what is being challenged.

_____
_____
_____
_____
_____

Envision a response that deals with the situation, and does so in a way that is consistent with your beliefs and the preferred future you have in mind for those involved.

_____
_____
_____
_____
_____

Execute the action and note the response.

_____
_____
_____
_____
_____

If you were doing it again, how would you do it differently?

Mahatma Gandhi

Gandhi revolutionized the lives of his fellow countrymen with a series of powerful signals. After a legal career in South Africa, he returned to India in 1915 and encountered unbelievable poverty, a rigid caste system and a lack of political will to overthrow India's colonial status. At his first meeting with the Indian Congress Party, he noticed that no Untouchables were invited as delegates. Their only function was to clean the latrines, an act thought too demeaning for anyone but Untouchables. Gandhi deliberately took a brush and began to clean the latrines himself, an act that sent shock waves through the party and through India's society at large.

Gandhi saw that village life, where 80 percent of the people lived, had to be rehabilitated. Village craftsmen had disappeared, unable to compete with cheaper mass-produced imports. Without a market for crafts there was no employment and, thus, no source of income for villagers. Gandhi believed that if India returned to a pre-industrial economy, at least the villagers wouldn't starve. To signal his intent, Gandhi spun his own cloth and urged followers to wear only clothing made by hand.

Throughout the 1920s he led protest movements and a peasant tax strike, always remaining centered on his value of non-violence despite the fact that it didn't come easily to him. Perhaps his most celebrated protest was the long Salt March in 1930. The signal he planned was to be a cumulative one. It was illegal for Indians to make their own salt — a ridiculous law symptomatic of the excesses of Imperialism. Gandhi announced that he would march to the sea and make his own salt, thus breaking the law. He walked 241 miles leading a procession that numbered in the thousands. In the eyes of observers it became almost a mystical event. People all around the world followed the slow deliberate progress of this little man in his home-spun dhoti. The action itself was simple; the visibility grew with each passing day, as did the power of Gandhi's signal.

As Nehru, India's first Prime Minister, said, "Gandhi had a curious knack for doing the right thing at the right psychological moment." Remaining consistent at all times was not natural for Gandhi. It required enormous self-discipline and a continuous effort to remain centered.

Values
- equality and an end to the caste system
- religious tolerance
- sincere respect for one's opponent
- respect for the well being and dignity of humanity

Vision
- freedom from intolerance
- a disciplined self-supporting people

Signals
- cleaning latrines
- spinning his own garment cloth (dhoti)
- the Salt March
- consistency of his behavior

Appropriate Leader Response to Challenge
- Whenever violence flared up, Gandhi urged a return to non-violence. During the bloodbath following the partitioning of India and Pakistan, Gandhi fasted until violence ceased.

6

Next Steps: Maintaining Perpetual Energy

So, where to from here? Hopefully your scrimmages produced enough evidence to convince you that *more* leadership or energy catalysts positioned throughout all levels of your organization could return great dividends. If so, it's time to expand your corporate energy initiative and get everyone involved. It won't be easy. It is a collaborative effort that can't be achieved alone. Everyone in your organization must be drawn in. But the rewards in terms of performance, profit, and excitement are well worth the effort.

I want to emphasize once again that the experiments you've been through deal only with leadership and the creation of energy. Management — the rational side of enterprise — must also be present before superior performance can occur. Healthy organizations also need planning, staffing, directing and controlling. But their correct place is in the turbulence. If you try to bring management's logic and precision in to your "I," it won't work. Practice good management, but don't let the mechanics take over. You have to embody your values and vision, and your best connection to other people is through signals — not systems. Live the paradox and move freely between your center and the turbulence. Never was it more crucial to "be in the right place at the right time."

My notions about creating corporate energy revolve around a few fundamental beliefs:

- Experiences that come from encouraging challenge and providing effective leader responses represent the most effective means of human learning.

- People will support emotionally only what they have had a hand in shaping.

- Education is to knowledge as training is to skill.

I believe training to be the ultimate corporate signal. If employees are sent to academic institutions, or if internal learning programs are theory-oriented, the message is clear: "We want you to know more, not necessarily do more." (See Chapter 7.)

Learning from the Experience of Others

Organizations that have succeeded in creating — and sustaining — energy did so because leaders made it happen. These leaders are not all charismatic, they are not a breed apart from the rest of us mortals. They are *people* obsessed with sharing their mental picture of a preferred future, signaling it visibly and actively. Devising and sending those signals becomes the number one priority of each working day. Tasks deemed to be essential aspects of the senior manager's job by many of us are delegated to others or pushed aside. They make time for signaling — come hell or high water. Successful leaders have faced challenges and hurdles all along the way, as will you. The following are the reflections of several executives who successfuly experimented with creating corporate energy and went on to make it part of their organization's culture.

Don't Ever Let It Die

There is no such thing as too simple a message about core values and vision. And no such thing as too much repetition.

Beware of the Time Lag

Creating energy normally starts with senior management who will work on the process long before most employees are aware of it. The sad truth is that at about the time senior management is getting sick of repeating values and vision, employees at the working levels are just starting to hear about it. Advertising professionals cope with this syndrome all the time. They spend months creating, planning and guiding a new campaign through early launch stages, and invariably when they start getting sick of the whole campaign, the public is just starting to sit up and take notice. That's the point where an imaginative relaunch is needed to rekindle senior management enthusiasm. The formal leader plays a crucial role in coping with this phenomenon.

Shallow Commitment

Initial enthusiasm can easily pass for acceptance, but after a few months you may find no new energy being generated. Middle managers, and even senior executives, will say "I understand." They'll even genuinely embrace the values and vision, but what they are usually missing is the ability to signal them. Typically, they know what role others should play in moving the organization closer to vision and values but when it comes to personal actions on their part, many managers can't express anything concrete beyond bland generalities which, of course, are non-actionable. This is especially true if the value represents a real change in the organization's culture. All you can do is keep signaling, until the light goes on for them — till they get the picture.

Values and vision tend to be lofty and idealistic — they have to be in order to generate energy — but that also makes it difficult for employees to translate them into their busy day-to-day jobs.

Don't Be Afraid to Be a Little Hokey
Your signals must be in character, things you're comfortable with, but it's the unusual that catches the organization's imagination. Do things that are different; the more unusual they are the more visible they'll be.

Publicize, Publicize, Publicize
Many organizations are too closed-mouthed about where they are going and what they believe in. Senior executives feel embarrassed and unprofessional saying that they believe in service or respect for people. The truth is, you can talk all you like and send all the signals you can, but employees really start to believe when your message is fed back to them from people outside the organization, neighbors or friends for instance.

Don't Be Afraid to Take Some Big Risks
Executives suffer from risk aversion. Business schools train us to minimize risk. But to exemplify your values and vision there are times when you need to be more innovative than usual. Push the limits once you are focused, when you know where you are going and what you believe in.

Get Middle Management Involved
Because of their role, middle managers are the ones who

have the responsibility for transforming the content of your "I" into the action plans of those who do the real work. If they're not with you 100 percent, your energy initiatives will never get past them. They may see the proposed changes as threatening. Their power is being removed when you attempt to energize others. You have to be prepared to invest a great deal of time to help them past this block.

Taking Time Saves Time

As you spread values and vision through the organization there will always be those who resist or whose commitment is soft. The cardinal sin is to manage around them and expect that they'll get on board eventually. Their resistance can spread as they will unintentionally attract others to their side. Take the time to personally confront every resister. Recognize that when they disagree with you there is usually a reason — a valid one to them. Sit down and find out what the real issues are. It actually saves time to take the time to do it, because if negative attitudes spread you may have to start all over again.

Danger Free

To establish the trust needed to make vision and values happen you have to promise people a danger-free environment where they can experiment with new ways of doing things and say whatever they like without fear of repercussions. Intellectually it's easy to agree to such a strategy. But it's going to slip — and it usually happens at middle management. When it does happen you must be prepared to react quickly. From the beginning, be candid and remind employees that everybody is human. Let them know that there will be lapses but that you're fully committed to seeing a danger-free work environment happen. Show them that you're obsessed with it. It's the only way.

300-percent Training

Momentum doesn't last forever. Middle management usually runs out of interest quicker than work teams or senior executives because they're used to living through short-term fixes that were a part of management development during the 60s and 70s. They're programmed to expect that the organization will lose interest and swing to a new fad before they are faced with having to follow through with the old one. Their mental muscles are trained in such a way that they don't have the discipline to maintain energy day after day.

You must get them to keep going back to the basics — again and again. One hundred percent training isn't enough. Three times through the organization and you start to get commitment and understanding at all levels. Most people will not get your message the first time around. And most companies don't put enough resource power behind training to get beyond that first go-around. They figure that once should be enough. Remember, "Knowing is not doing."

Follow Up Quickly

The first time you open up communication with front-line people you may not get a clear set of benchmarks about where you stand with them. More likely you'll get an emotional burst of pent-up frustration. But it's important to hear them out and get back to them again. And quickly. The second time you'll get better feedback and crisper suggestions because if you've stayed centered they will have begun to trust you. You'll get a much truer reading of the corporate pulse after the first time out.

When you get out from behind your desk to meet employees their initial responses may be very traditional, staid and proper. By the second time around you will notice that even senior officers start putting a little more razzma-

tazz into the process. They will become more vocal in cele-
brations, and celebration is a key word. By the third time,
as the Japanese have found, people start to hear with their
hearts as well as with their heads. Until your values and
vision have worked their way down to the front line, until
foremen and supervisors are willing to fight their managers to defend their "I" you don't really have it.

Ownership Is Important

Put yourself on the leading edge in your industry for quality, service — or whatever will make impact — and keep
yourself there. Once you've found your own niche, pride
takes over. The process starts to fuel itself. Employees start
recognizing that values and vision are not just another hare-
brained scheme that will blow away with the first wind.
They'll begin to suspect that your theme is here to stay.
And if they've had a hand in putting it there, if you have
given them a sense of ownership, they'll keep it going for
you. Once ownership is in place you get consistency.

Selective Memory

The results of your values and vision will crop up where
you least expect them. Employees will most energetically
remember values when it suits their argument. For example, if you have to fire an employee, other staff will question
your "respect for the individual." But respecting people
doesn't mean you should not fire non-performers or not be
critical of them in performance reviews. If anything, respect for co-workers who've been carrying the sub-par
performer should entice you to take firm action. Selective
memory is frustrating. But see each occurrence as a challenge that provides an excellent opportunity to reconfirm
and translate your values into concrete working terms for
employees who can't see beyond the words.

Despite frustrations and setbacks, when asked about what went better than they expected, the most common findings of participating executives was that the committed response from their organization happened much faster than they had initially expected it would.

To give effective feedback you must be specific. I have found that you should separate the performance from the person, recognize the act, not the individual. For instance, if an appliance store manager saw an employee providing particularly good service to a customer, he or she would refer to the specific observed behavior, saying, "When I saw you satisfying the customer's concerns about whether this stereo would fit with his other components, I felt you were living our service value well." Had circumstances called for a negative response, he might have said, "When I saw you and that customer walk away from each other, I felt you let our service value down. Perhaps if you had shown a little more concern for the customer's needs he might have responded more favorably."

Martin Luther King, Jr.

For more than a decade, Martin Luther King played a leading role in the struggle for black American equality. He attracted a large following that cut across racial lines. Through speeches and other visible acts, he communicated to white America the need to end segregation, and to his followers, the importance of non-violence.

He learned early in his career to convert foes into allies. While studying divinity at Crozer Seminary in Pennsylvania, a white student, whose room had been vandalized, blamed King. The student, well known for his racist views, pulled a gun and threatened to kill King. King remained calm and denied having any involvement until eventually the student was disarmed. King refused to press charges and in time won the friendship of the white student.

In the mid-50s, he abandoned plans to become a university professor and returned to his Southern home to join the protest movement against discrimination. He came to prominence in 1956 when he spearheaded a Montgomery, Alabama boycott after a black woman was arrested for refusing to sit in the back of a bus.

From that point on, he faced constant threats but, as a signal to others, he gave up keeping a gun in his house. King alternated between participating in protest marches and sit-ins in the South and making speeches in northern parts of America. Although there were many victories, each step forward produced little tangible evidence of change, creating frustration among his followers. King countered the increasing violence against blacks by stepping up his personal exposure. His followers often tried to draw him into confrontations that were not in keeping with his value of non-violence.

In 1963, there were 930 demonstrations in 115 cities, 288 communities where bi-racial committees were negotiating change, and 20,000 people jailed. To cap this drive, King marched on Washington where he delivered his unforgettable "I have a dream" speech. Toward the end of his life, he broadened his scope to include the poor and downtrodden of all races.

Values
- the brotherhood of mankind
- peaceful, non-violent change
- laws conforming to morality
- the dignity of people

Vision
- equality for all. "From every mountaintop, let freedom ring."

Signals
- giving up his gun despite repeated death threats
- protest marches, sit-ins and demonstrations
- his calm, controlled behavior in the face of personal danger

Appropriate Leader Response to Challenge
- refusing to be drawn into demonstrations that did not fit his values and vision
- approving the use of troops in 1967 to control black rioters in Newark and Detroit. He suffered politically, but held to his ideals of non-violence.

7

Training for Energized Organizations

Corporate energy is created by individuals with enough leadership to act as catalysts. They start a chain reaction in the organization. The more catalysts you have transmitting values and vision, the greater the amount of energy produced. Such leadership does not just happen. Formal and informal training processes are the primary corporate tools available to transform values and vision into meaningful results. To have impact, training must:

Have a Clear Goal
Senior executives must be absolutely clear about what training is needed to move the organization closer to their vision, values and business plan. The aim should be to provide practical skills that can be immediately used in the job of transforming values and vision into day-to-day tasks. The concern should be with action plans.

Generate Enthusiastic Involvement

Too often, senior management truly believes it is giving total support to training, while people involved in training functions believe they are receiving very little. Intentionally or otherwise, your personal involvement signals how you want employees to view training. Let them *see* that you consider it as vital. It is the planned means to achieve sought-after goals. Get employees to try visioning what an ideal training experience would be like.

Be Skills-Based, Not Theoretical

Avoid training that is esoteric or theoretical. Aim for skill training. Remember, employees already know more than they are doing. The emphasis must be on practical skills that employees can use tomorrow.

Produce a Sense of Urgency

In formal education, reflection and introspection are important. But if you want to create energy, the training process must be action-oriented and infused with a sense of urgency.

Maintain Consistent Quality

The quality of training should be of the highest order for all sectors of your organization, year in and year out. Don't forget those at distant locations. You'll be creating your own barriers to energy if new employees, those nearing retirement, or other employee groups are left out.

Achieve Critical Mass

Since you want to involve every employee in creating energy, training must involve everyone in a planned top-down, bottom-up activity. It should not be an activity reserved for an occasional middle manager who has earned a perk. Peter Drucker claims that 30 percent of a group must be trained before any meaningful impact will be felt. The larger the numbers the greater that impact will be.

Evaluate, Results

Re-examine your training constantly. Ask for feedback from all levels. Signal that you expect each step to move the organization closer to your values, vision and plan.

Training is the ultimate organizational signal. Use it to let employees know what is strategically relevant *now*. Providing a stress management course may well be a humane gesture, but is it the most relevant signal you can send to your organization about what is important to you? To implement change and capitalize on new horizons employees must develop their interactive and professional skills.

Enthusiasm and excitement are great fuel but to fully capitalize on your change initiative, four levels of skills must be developed before employees can work together as a talented, energized team. Skills help employees function while in the turbulence. It also shows them how to give and receive the support that comes from knowing how to use their "I" of the hurricane.

The following list identifies four sets of interactive skills that are needed to produce and maintain corporate energy:

Personal Skills
1. Working smarter rather than harder
2. Dealing with change
3. Being a team player
4. Giving feedback to help others
5. Taking on new assignments
6. Responding positively to negative situations

8

Conclusion

"Thinking is easy, acting is difficult. To put one's thoughts into action is the most difficult thing in the world."
Goethe

Action need not be difficult. Once you arm yourself with a mental picture of a preferred future (vision) and a set of obsessive beliefs (core values) that a majority of the people in your organization share, you need only remember:

- to consistently signal your intent using visible actions
- welcome challenge by responding with behavior that not only solves the problem but further reinforces where you are going (vision) and what you believe in (core values)

Taking action can be difficult — if you spend time thinking about it. Instead of imagining all the potential problems that action (or the lack of it) could cause, focus instead on the power you already have as a leader to affect the energy of every employee. Imagine positive results:

- a mindset, shared by all employees, that produces superb quality, day in and day out
- a stream of innovative solutions coming from your own people that keeps your organization competitive
- customers complimenting your employees for really knowing how to listen and how to provide excellent service
- people working smarter as well as harder and breaking all productivity records

People want to make a personal contribution and belong to something worthwhile. Remember, *you* can be the catalyst that unleashes the unlimited reserves of energy currently lying dormant in your organization.

Appendix

If this book has done its job it has altered the way you think about yourself in relation to your organization. You may find the following personal assessment useful. When reading these statements, reflect on how your answer is different from what it might have been before you read THE ENERGY FACTOR: HOW TO MOTIVATE YOUR WORKFORCE.

Questionnaire: Creating or Destroying Energy

Read the following statements and circle the response closest to your own position from 1 = strongly disagree, through 4 = agree, to 7 = strongly agree.

1. The bottom line can be impacted as much by executive coaching and cheerleading as by rules, policy and procedure.
   1   2   3   4   5   6   7

2. Quality should be a value, not a control system.
   1   2   3   4   5   6   7

3. In today's competitive business environment, intuition is just as important as planning and financial analysis.
   1   2   3   4   5   6   7

4. Visioning is just as relevant as strategic planning in preparing an organization for the future.
   1   2   3   4   5   6   7

5. Productivity need not suffer by the removal of "time clocks" and other control systems.
   1   2   3   4   5   6   7

6. Employee attitude, not automation, is the key to enhanced productivity.
   1   2   3   4   5   6   7

7. Employees contribute best when they believe that the organization's leader is taking them someplace worthwhile.
   1   2   3   4   5   6   7

Questionnaire: Core Values

Read the following statements and circle the response closest to your own position from 1 = strongly disagree, through 4 = agree, to 7 = strongly agree.

1. I can summarize in a couple of sentences things that I (and most of my people) believe in.
   1   2   3   4   5   6   7

2. We have documented clearly what our organization's core values are.
   1   2   3   4   5   6   7

3. An organization's core values are uncovered, not created.
   1   2   3   4   5   6   7

4. Core values, like external advertising, should be heart-felt and uplifting to employees.
   1   2   3   4   5   6   7

5. The presence of negative energy can help pinpoint the presence of an unsatisfied core value.
   1   2   3   4   5   6   7

6. We test our management decisions and actions against a set of core values.
   1   2   3   4   5   6   7

7. Values not only contribute to employee morale, but have a direct impact on the bottom line.
   1   2   3   4   5   6   7

Questionnaire: Vision

Read the following statements and circle the response closest to your own position from 1 = strongly disagree, through 4 = agree, to 7 = strongly agree.

1. As well as our business plans, an inspirational vision of a preferred future guides the direction of our organization.
   1   2   3   4   5   6   7

2. I have a mental picture of what our organization could look like in 5–10 years.
   1   2   3   4   5   6   7

3. I regularly articulate to others what I feel our organization can become.
   1   2   3   4   5   6   7

4. Goals alone do not provide sufficient purpose to bind a group of people together as a productive team.
   1   2   3   4   5   6   7

5. The bottom line can be impacted as much by a mental picture of "how things could be" as by a detailed plan.
   1   2   3   4   5   6   7

6. The ability to dream is an essential part of leadership.
   1   2   3   4   5   6   7

7. Vision produces energy, whereas goals provide direction.
   1   2   3   4   5   6   7

Questionnaire: Signaling Skills

Read the following statements and circle the response closest to your own position from 1 = strongly disagree, through 4 = agree, to 7 = strongly agree.

1. I take care to always do what I say.
   1   2   3   4   5   6   7

2. Explaining the rationale of my decision making to staff is as important as the decision itself.
   1   2   3   4   5   6   7

3. Good managers lead by personal example.
   1   2   3   4   5   6   7

4. I reflect on my actions and decisions to ensure that they have been consistent with our core values.
   1   2   3   4   5   6   7

5. I get out of my office and make a special effort to find and recognize people doing the right things the right way.
   1   2   3   4   5 . 6   7

6. Last month I spent at least 1/3 of my time contacting clients, employees and suppliers.
   1   2   3   4   5   6   7

7. Employees who have not formally read about our organization's values would nonetheless have a pretty good idea what they were.
   1   2   3   4   5   6   7

Questionnaire: Challenge

Read the following statements and circle the response closest to your own position from 1 = strongly disagree, through 4 = agree, to 7 = strongly agree.

1. The presence of unsanctioned projects does not concern me.
   1   2   3   4   5   6   7

2. I always speak positively about consumer groups and government regulations.
   1   2   3   4   5   6   7

3. Diversity of thought and opinion among members of a management team renders them more effective.
   1   2   3   4   5   6   7

4. I hold people who do not challenge my orders in lower regard than those who do.
   1   2   3   4   5   6   7

5. I can list ten occasions when I have encouraged others to act as devil's advocates.
   1   2   3   4   5   6   7

6. I would not be afraid to positively recognize someone whose attempted new action met with failure.
   1   2   3   4   5   6   7

7. The presence or absence of vision and values determines an organization's capacity to manage change.
   1   2   3   4   5   6   7

Questionnaire: Appropriate Leader Response

Read the following statements and circle the response closest to your own position from 1 = strongly disagree, through 4 = agree, to 7 = strongly agree.

1. During crises, I take pains to ensure that my actions reflect as much as possible the organization's values.
   1   2   3   4   5   6   7

2. The threat of a costly strike need not deter an organization from living up to its core values.
   1   2   3   4   5   6   7

3. I seldom find myself making decisions that contradict earlier ones made under similar circumstances.
   1   2   3   4   5   6   7

4. I often modify proposed decisions to reflect more directly our vision and/or values.
   1   2   3   4   5   6   7

5. Sometimes I use "show biz" to focus attention on important decisions.
   1   2   3   4   5   6   7

6. When I analyse the effects of decisions I have made under pressure, they often reveal short-term sacrifice for long-term gain.
   1   2   3   4   5   6   7

7. People are positively motivated by most of my decisions and actions.
   1   2   3   4   5   6   7

Piatkus Business Books

Piatkus Business Books have been created for people like you, busy executives and managers who need expert knowledge readily available in a clear and easy-to-follow format. All the books are written by specialists in their field. They will help you improve your skills quickly and effortlessly in the workplace and on a personal level.

Each book is packed with ideas and good advice which can be put into practice immediately. Titles include:

General Management Skills

Be Your Own PR Expert   Bill Penn
Brain Power: The 12-Week Mental Training Programme   Marilyn vos Savant and Leonore Fleischer
The Complete Time Management System   Christian H. Godefroy and John Clark
Confident Decision Making   J. Edward Russo and Paul J. H. Schoemaker
Dealing with Difficult People   Roberta Cava
The Energy Factor: How to Motivate Your Workforce   Art McNeil
Firing On All Cylinders: Tried and Tested Techniques to Improve the Performance of Your Organisation   Jim Clemmer with Barry Sheehy
How to Develop and Profit from Your Creative Powers   Michael LeBoeuf
The Influential Manager: How to Use Company Politics Constructively   Lee Bryce
Leadership Skills for Every Manager   Jim Clemmer and Art McNeil
Managing Your Team   John Spencer and Adrian Pruss
Play to Your Strengths: Focus on What You Do Well – and Success Will Follow   Donald O. Clifton and Paula Nelson
Problem Solving Techniques that Really Work   Malcolm Bird
Psychological Testing for Managers: A Complete Guide to Using and Surviving 19 Popular Recruitment and Career Development Tests   Dr Stephanie Jones
Your Memory: How It Works and How to Improve It   Kenneth L. Higbee

Sales and Customer Services

The Art of the Hard Sell   Robert L. Shook
How to Close Every Sale   Joe Girard
How to Succeed in Network Marketing   Leonard S. Hawkins
How to Win Customers and Keep Them for Life   Michael LeBoeuf
Sales Power: The Silva Mind Method for Sales Professionals   José Silva and Ed Bernd Jnr
Selling by Direct Mail   John W. Graham and Susan K. Jones
The Selling Edge: Tactics for Winning a Sale Every Time   Patrick Forsyth
Telephone Selling Techniques that Really Work   Bill Good

Presentation and Communication

Better Business Writing   Maryann V. Piotrowski
The Complete Book of Business Etiquette   Lynne Brennan and David Block
Confident Conversation: How to Talk in any Business or Social Situation   Dr Lillian Glass
Personal Power: How to Achieve Influence and Success in Your Professional Life   Philippa Davies
Powerspeak: The Complete Guide to Public Speaking and Communication   Dorothy Leeds
Confident Speaking: How to Communicate Effectively Using the Power Talk System   Christian H. Godefroy and Stephanie Barrat
Say What You Mean and Get What You Want: How to Speak the Language of Success   George R. Walther
Your Total Image: How to Communicate Success   Philippa Davies

Careers

The Influential Woman: How to Achieve Success Without Losing Your Femininity   Lee Bryce
Marketing Yourself: How to Sell Yourself and Get the Jobs You've Always Wanted   Dorothy Leeds
Networking and Mentoring: A Woman's Guide   Dr Lily Segerman-Peck
The Perfect CV   Tom Jackson
10 Steps to the Top   Marie Jennings
Which Way Now? How to Plan and Develop a Successful Career   Bridget Wright

Small Business

The Best Person for the Job   Malcolm Bird
Making Profits: A 6-Month Action Plan for the Small Business   Malcolm Bird

You too can benefit from expert advice. For a free brochure with further information on our complete range of business titles, please write to:

Piatkus Books
Freepost 7 (WD 4505)
London W1E 4EZ

PIATKUS